COOKSHELF
Chinese

Jenny Stacey

DP
DEMPSEY
PARR

First published in Great Britain in 1998 by
Dempsey Parr
13 Whiteladies Road
Clifton
Bristol BS8 1PB

ISBN: 1-84084-291-1

Produced by Haldane Mason, London

Acknowledgements
Art Director: Ron Samuels
Editorial Director: Sydney Francis
Managing Editor: Jo-Anne Cox
Design: dap ltd
Photography: Andrew Sydenham
Home Economist: Kathryn Hawkins
Home Economist's Assistant: Eliza Baird

Colour Reproduction by
Inka Graphics, Cardiff

Printed in China

Note
Cup measurements in this book are for American cups.
Tablespoons are assumed to be 15 ml. Unless otherwise stated,
milk is assumed to be full fat, eggs are medium and pepper is freshly
ground black pepper.

Contents

Introduction

In the West we tend to talk about Chinese cooking as a generalization, as though it were the same throughout China. In fact, China is a vast country, with a range of topography and climates that produce distinct regional differences.

This book, contains recipes that are popular in both China and the West. Dishes from Szechuan in the West, Canton in the South, Beijing in the North and Shanghai in the East offer an array of different flavours and cooking methods. The dishes included in this book range from hot and spicy to delicate flavours using fish and vegetables, with a mid-range of sweet-and-sour dishes, rice, noodles and a small section of desserts.

One of the most important features of Chinese cooking is texture. Vegetables should remain crisp, and rice and noodles should be treated like pasta and retain their 'bite' after cooking. Ingredients such as tofu (bean curd) are used for texture, even though they have little flavour. Bamboo shoots, a common ingredient, are included purely for texture.

Although the Chinese make use of fresh foods, they also use dried foodstuffs in their recipes, in particular mushrooms, tofu (bean curd), noodles and spices.

COOKING METHODS

The Chinese combine a couple of cooking methods in one dish, such as steaming and then frying, or frying and roasting, but little special equipment is required.

Steaming is widely used in Chinese cookery. Traditionally bamboo steamers are used, so that a whole meal may be cooked in one stack of bamboo racks. The rice is usually placed in the bottom and different dishes stacked on top, those taking the longest to cook being placed at the bottom. If you do not have a steamer, invert a heatproof plate in a large saucepan and cover it with a lid or foil. Boiling water is added to the steamer, to cover one third of the depth of the dish. This water may need topping up during cooking, although many of the dishes cook very quickly. Steaming is a very healthy method of cooking, not using any fat, and it traps the flavours of the dish.

Stir-frying is done in a wok that must be heated before use. Foods of similar size (all small) are stirred constantly, so that as they come into contact with the wok, they cook quickly. Sometimes foods are cooked in batches and removed. This is to preserve flavours. The dishes are always brought together in the wok at the end of cooking and may have sauces added during or at the end of the cooking time, depending on the region from which they originated. Peanut oil is usually used for stir-frying, but vegetable oil may be used in its place.

Deep-frying is also done in the wok, which uses less oil than a deep-fryer. The shape of the wok allows oil to drain from the food into the centre of the wok. The foods are often marinated first or coated in a light batter. Quick-frying is also used, whereby foods are either fried on one side (used for noodles) and not turned or turned once and sliced for serving.

USEFUL CHINESE INGREDIENTS

Bamboo shoots *These are added for texture, as they have very little flavour. Available in cans, they are a common ingredient in Chinese cooking.*

Beansprouts *These are mung bean shoots, which are very nutritious, containing many vitamins. They add crunch to a recipe and are widely available. Do not overcook them, as they wilt and do not add texture to the dish.*

Black beans *These are soy beans and are very salty. They can be bought and crushed with salt and then rinsed or used in the form of a ready-made sauce for convenience.*

Chinese beans *These long beans may be eaten whole and are very tender. French (green) beans may also be used.*

Chinese five spice powder *An aromatic blend of cinnamon, cloves, star anise, fennel and brown peppercorns. It is often used in marinades.*

Chinese leaves *A light green leaf with a sweet flavour. It can be found readily in most supermarkets.*

Hoisin sauce *A dark brown, sweet, thick sauce that is widely available. It is made from spices, soy sauce, garlic and chilli and is often served as a dipping sauce.*

Lychees *These are worth buying fresh, as they are easy to prepare. Inside the inedible skin is a fragrant white fruit. Lychees are available canned and are a classic ingredient.*

Mango *Choose a ripe mango for its sweet, scented flesh. If a mango is underripe when bought, leave it in a sunny place for a few days before using.*

Noodles *The Chinese use several varieties of noodle. You will probably find it easier to use the readily available dried varieties, such as egg noodles, which are yellow, rice stick noodles, which are white and very fine, or transparent noodles, which are opaque when dry and turn transparent on cooking. However, cellophane or rice noodles may be used instead.*

Oyster sauce *Readily available, this sauce is made from oysters, salt, seasonings and cornflour (cornstarch) and is brown in colour.*

Pak choi *Also known as Chinese cabbage, this has a mild, slightly bitter flavour.*

Rice vinegar *This has a mild, sweet taste that is quite delicate. It is available in some supermarkets, but if not available use cider vinegar instead.*

Rice wine *This is similar to dry sherry in colour, alcohol content and smell, but it is worth buying rice wine for its distinctive flavour.*

Sesame oil *This is made from roasted sesame seeds and has an intense flavour. It burns easily and is therefore added at the end of cooking for flavour, and is not used for frying.*

Soy sauce *This is widely available, but it is worth buying a good grade of sauce. It is produced in both light and dark varieties – the former is used with fish and vegetables for a lighter colour and flavour, while the latter, being darker, richer, saltier and more intense, is used as a dipping sauce or with strongly flavoured meats.*

Star anise *This is an eight-pointed, star-shaped pod with a strong aniseed flavour. The spice is also available ground. If a pod is added to a dish, it should be removed before serving.*

Szechuan pepper *This is quite hot and spicy and should be used sparingly. It is red in colour and is readily available.*

Tofu (bean curd) *This soya bean paste is available in several forms. The cake variety, which is soft and spongy and a white-grey colour, is used in this book. It is very bland, but adds texture to dishes and is perfect for absorbing all the other flavours in the dish.*

Water chestnuts *These are flat and round and can usually only be purchased in cans, already peeled. They add a delicious crunch to dishes and have a sweet flavour.*

Yellow beans *Again a soy bean and very salty. Use a variety that is chunky rather than smooth.*

5

Soups & Starters

In China soups are not usually served
at the beginning of a meal but between courses to
clear the palate. It is also quite common for Chinese
families to serve a large tureen of clear soup at the
same time as the other dishes. The soups in this
chapter bring a whole range of flavours and textures
to the table. There are thicker soups, thin clear
consommés and those topped with wontons for effect
and flavour. These soups can be eaten as a lunch or
snack on their own – whatever your preference,
they all taste delicious!

The starters in this chapter are a combination
of old favourites and traditional Chinese dishes,
and there is sure to be something to suit every
occasion. One of the advantages of these dishes is
that they can be prepared and cooked in advance.
Instead of serving the starters individually, try
serving a small portion of each together as an
assorted hors d'oeuvres. Remember not to have more
than one of the same type of food – the ingredients
should be chosen for their harmony and balance in
colour, aroma, flavour and texture.

Clear Chicken & Egg Soup

Serves 4

INGREDIENTS

1 tsp salt	1 leek, sliced	1 tbsp dry sherry
1 tbsp rice wine vinegar	125 g/4¹/₂ oz broccoli florets	dash of chilli sauce
4 eggs	125 g/4¹/₂ oz/1 cup shredded	chilli powder, to garnish
850 ml/1¹/₂ pints/3³/₄ cups	cooked chicken	
chicken stock	2 open-cap mushrooms, sliced	

1 Bring a large saucepan of water to the boil and add the salt and rice wine vinegar. Reduce the heat so that it is just simmering and carefully break the eggs into the water, one at a time. Poach the eggs for 1 minute. Remove the poached eggs with a slotted spoon and set aside.

2 Bring the stock to the boil in a separate pan and add the leek, broccoli, chicken, mushrooms and sherry and season with chilli sauce to taste. Cook for 10–15 minutes.

3 Add the poached eggs to the soup and cook for a further 2 minutes. Carefully transfer the soup and poached eggs to 4 individual soup bowls. Dust with a little chilli powder to garnish and serve immediately.

COOK'S TIP

You could use 4 dried Chinese mushrooms, rehydrated according to the packet instructions, instead of the open-cap mushrooms, if you prefer.

VARIATION

You could substitute 125 g/4¹/₂ oz fresh or canned crabmeat or the same quantity of fresh or frozen cooked prawns (shrimp) for the chicken, if desired.

Curried Chicken & Sweetcorn (Corn) Soup

Serves 4

INGREDIENTS

175 g/6 oz can sweetcorn
(corn), drained
850 ml/1½ pints/3¾ cups
chicken stock
350 g/12 oz cooked, lean
chicken, cut into strips

16 baby corn cobs
1 tsp Chinese curry powder
1-cm/½-inch piece fresh root
ginger (ginger root), grated

3 tbsp light soy sauce
2 tbsp chopped chives

1 Place the canned sweetcorn (corn) in a food processor, together with 150 ml/¼ pint/⅔ cup of the chicken stock and process until the mixture forms a smooth purée.

2 Pass the sweetcorn purée through a fine sieve, pressing with the back of a spoon to remove any husks.

3 Pour the remaining chicken stock into a large pan and add the strips of cooked chicken. Stir in the sweetcorn (corn) purée.

4 Add the baby corn cobs and bring the soup to the boil. Boil the soup for 10 minutes.

5 Add the curry powder, ginger and soy sauce and cook for 10–15 minutes. Stir in the chives.

6 Transfer the soup to warm bowls and serve.

COOK'S TIP

Prepare the soup up to 24 hours in advance without adding the chicken, let cool, cover and store in the refrigerator. Add the chicken and heat the soup through thoroughly before serving.

Hot & Sour Soup

Serves 4

INGREDIENTS

2 tbsp cornflour (cornstarch)
4 tbsp water
2 tbsp light soy sauce
3 tbsp rice wine vinegar
$1/2$ tsp ground black pepper
1 small fresh red chilli, finely chopped

1 egg
2 tbsp vegetable oil
1 onion, chopped
850 ml/$1^1/2$ pints/$3^3/4$ cups chicken or beef consommé
1 open-cap mushroom, sliced

50 g/$1^3/4$ oz skinless chicken breast, cut into very thin strips
1 tsp sesame oil

1 Blend the cornflour (cornstarch) with the water to form a smooth paste. Add the soy sauce, rice wine vinegar, pepper and chilli and mix together.

2 Break the egg into a separate bowl and beat well.

3 Heat the oil in a preheated wok and fry the onion for 1–2 minutes.

4 Stir in the consommé, mushroom and chicken and bring to the boil. Cook for 15 minutes or until the chicken is tender.

5 Pour the cornflour (cornstarch) mixture into the soup and cook, stirring, until it thickens.

6 As you are stirring, gradually drizzle the egg into the soup, to create threads of egg.

7 Sprinkle with the sesame oil and serve immediately.

COOK'S TIP

Make sure that the egg is poured in very slowly and that you stir continuously to create threads of egg and not large pieces.

Peking Duck Soup

Serves 4

> **INGREDIENTS**
>
> 125 g/4¹/₂ oz lean duck breast meat
> 225 g/8 oz Chinese leaves (cabbage)
>
> 850 ml/1¹/₂ pints/3³/₄ cups chicken or duck stock
> 1 tbsp dry sherry or rice wine
> 1 tbsp light soy sauce
> 2 garlic cloves, crushed
>
> pinch of ground star anise
> 1 tbsp sesame seeds
> 1 tsp sesame oil
> 1 tbsp chopped fresh parsley

1 Remove the skin from the duck breast and finely dice the flesh.

2 Using a sharp knife, shred the Chinese leaves (cabbage).

3 Put the stock in a large saucepan and bring to the boil.

4 Add the sherry or rice wine, soy sauce, diced duck meat and shredded Chinese leaves and stir to mix thoroughly. Reduce the heat and leave to simmer for 15 minutes.

5 Stir in the garlic and star anise and cook over a low heat for 10–15 minutes, or until the duck is tender.

6 Dry-fry the sesame seeds in a preheated, heavy-based frying pan (skillet) or wok, stirring.

7 Remove the sesame seeds from the pan and stir them into the soup, together with the sesame oil and parsley.

8 Spoon the soup into warm bowls and serve.

COOK'S TIP

If Chinese leaves (cabbage) are unavailable, use leafy green cabbage instead. You may wish to adjust the quantity to taste, as Western cabbage has a stronger flavour and odour than Chinese leaves (cabbage).

Beef & Vegetable Noodle Soup

Serves 4

INGREDIENTS

225 g/8 oz lean beef	1 tsp sesame oil	1/2 leek, shredded
1 garlic clove, crushed	225 g/8 oz egg noodles	125 g/4 1/2 oz broccoli, cut
2 spring onions (scallions),	850 ml/1 1/2 pints/3 3/4 cups	into florets (flowerets)
chopped	beef stock	pinch of chilli powder
3 tbsp soy sauce	3 baby corn cobs, sliced	

1 Using a sharp knife, cut the beef into thin strips and place them in a shallow glass bowl.

2 Add the garlic, spring onions (scallions), soy sauce and sesame oil and mix together well, turning the beef to coat. Cover and leave to marinate in the refrigerator for 30 minutes.

3 Cook the noodles in a saucepan of boiling water for 3–4 minutes. Drain the noodles thoroughly and set aside until required.

4 Put the beef stock in a large saucepan and bring to the boil.

5 Add the beef, together with the marinade, the baby corn, leek and broccoli. Cover and leave to simmer over a low heat for 7–10 minutes, or until the beef and vegetables are tender and cooked through.

6 Stir in the noodles and chilli powder and cook for a further 2–3 minutes. Transfer to bowls and serve immediately.

COOK'S TIP

Vary the vegetables used, or use those to hand. If preferred, use a few drops of chilli sauce instead of chilli powder, but remember it is very hot!

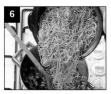

Lamb & Rice Soup

Serves 4

INGREDIENTS

150 g/5¹/₂ oz lean lamb	1 leek, sliced	1 medium open-cap
50 g/1³/₄ oz/¹/₄ cup rice	1 garlic clove, thinly sliced	mushroom, thinly sliced
850 ml/1¹/₂ pints/3³/₄ cups	2 tsp light soy sauce	salt
lamb stock	1 tsp rice wine vinegar	

1 Using a sharp knife, trim any fat from the lamb and cut the meat into thin strips. Set aside until required.

2 Bring a large pan of lightly salted water to the boil and add the rice. Bring back to the boil, stir once, reduce the heat and cook for 10–15 minutes, until tender. Drain, rinse under cold running water, drain again and set aside until required.

3 Meanwhile, put the lamb stock in a large saucepan and bring to the boil.

4 Add the lamb strips, leek, garlic, soy sauce and rice wine vinegar to the stock in the pan. Reduce the heat, cover and leave to simmer for 10 minutes, or until the lamb is tender and cooked through.

5 Add the mushroom slices and the rice to the pan and cook for a further 2–3 minutes, or until the mushroom is completely cooked through.

6 Ladle the soup into 4 individual warmed soup bowls and serve immediately.

COOK'S TIP

Use a few dried Chinese mushrooms, rehydrated according to the packet instructions and chopped, as an alternative to the open-cap mushroom. Add the Chinese mushrooms with the lamb in step 4.

Fish Soup with Wontons

Serves 4

INGREDIENTS

125 g/4¹/2 oz large, cooked,
   peeled prawns (shrimp)
1 tsp chopped chives
1 small garlic clove, finely
   chopped
1 tbsp vegetable oil

12 wonton wrappers
1 small egg, beaten
850 ml/1¹/2 pints/3³/4 cups
   fish stock
175 g/6 oz white fish fillet,
   diced

dash of chilli sauce
sliced fresh red chilli and
   chives, to garnish

1 Roughly chop a quarter of the prawns (shrimp) and mix together with the chopped chives and garlic.

2 Heat the oil in a preheated wok and stir-fry the prawn (shrimp) mixture for 1–2 minutes. Remove from the heat and set aside to cool completely.

3 Spread out the wonton wrappers on a work surface (counter). Spoon a little of the prawn (shrimp) filling into the centre of each wonton wrapper. Brush the edges of the wonton wrappers with beaten egg and press the edges together, scrunching them to form a 'moneybag' shape. Set aside while you are preparing the soup.

4 Pour the fish stock into a large saucepan and bring to the boil. Add the diced white fish and the remaining prawns (shrimp) and cook for 5 minutes.

5 Season to taste with the chilli sauce. Add the wontons and cook for a further 5 minutes. Spoon into warmed serving bowls, garnish with sliced red chilli and chives and serve immediately.

VARIATION

Replace the prawns (shrimp) with cooked crabmeat for an alternative flavour.

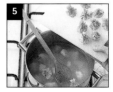

Crab & Ginger Soup

Serves 4

INGREDIENTS

1 carrot, chopped
1 leek, chopped
1 bay leaf
850 ml/1½ pints/3¾ cups
   fish stock

2 medium-sized cooked crabs
2.5-cm/1-inch piece fresh root
   ginger (ginger root), grated
1 tsp light soy sauce

½ tsp ground star anise
salt and pepper

1 Put the carrot, leek, bay leaf and stock into a large pan and bring to the boil. Reduce the heat, cover and simmer for 10 minutes, or until the vegetables are nearly tender.

2 Meanwhile, remove all of the meat from the cooked crabs. Break off the claws, break the joints and remove the meat (you may require a fork or skewer for this). Add the crabmeat to the saucepan of fish stock.

3 Add the ginger, soy sauce and star anise to the fish stock and bring to the boil. Leave to simmer for about 10 minutes, or until the vegetables are tender and the crab is heated through. Season.

4 Ladle the soup into warmed serving bowls and garnish with crab claws. Serve at once.

COOK'S TIP

If fresh crabmeat is unavailable, use drained canned crabmeat or thawed frozen crabmeat instead.

COOK'S TIP

To prepare cooked crab, loosen the meat from the shell by banging the back of the underside with a clenched fist. Stand the crab on its edge with the shell towards you. Force the shell from the body with your thumbs. Twist off the legs and claws and remove the meat. Twist off the tail; discard. Remove and discard the gills. Cut the body in half along the centre and remove the meat. Scoop the brown meat from the shell with a spoon.

Shrimp Dumpling Soup

Serves 4

INGREDIENTS

DUMPLINGS:
150 g/5^1/2 oz/1^5/8 cups plain
   (all-purpose) flour
50 ml/2 fl oz/^{1}/4 cup boiling
   water
25 ml/1 fl oz/^{1}/8 cup cold
   water
1^1/2 tsp vegetable oil

FILLING:
125 g/4^1/2 oz minced (ground)
   pork
125 g/4^1/2 oz cooked peeled
   shrimp, chopped
50 g/1^3/4 oz canned water
   chestnuts, drained, rinsed
   and chopped
1 celery stick, chopped
1 tsp cornflour (cornstarch)

1 tbsp sesame oil
1 tbsp light soy sauce

SOUP:
850 ml/1^1/2 pints/3^3/4 cups
   fish stock
50 g/1^3/4 oz cellophane
   noodles
1 tbsp dry sherry
chopped chives, to garnish

1 To make the dumplings, mix the flour, boiling water, cold water and oil in a bowl until a pliable dough is formed.

2 Knead the dough on a floured surface for 5 minutes. Cut the dough into 16 equal-sized pieces.

3 Roll the dough pieces into rounds 7.5 cm/ 3 inches in diameter.

4 Mix the filling ingredients together.

5 Spoon a little of the filling mixture into the centre of each round. Bring the edges of the dough together, scrunching them up to form a 'moneybag' shape. Twist to seal.

6 Pour the fish stock into a large saucepan and bring to the boil.

7 Add the cellophane noodles, dumplings and dry sherry to the pan and cook for 4–5 minutes, until the noodles and dumplings are tender. Garnish and serve.

COOK'S TIP

Wonton wrappers may be used instead of the dumpling dough if time is short.

Chinese Cabbage Soup

Serves 4

INGREDIENTS

450 g/1 lb pak choi	1 tbsp light soy sauce	1 tbsp cornflour (cornstarch)
600 ml/1 pint/2^1/2 cups	1 tbsp caster (superfine) sugar	2 tbsp water
vegetable stock	1 tbsp dry sherry	
1 tbsp rice wine vinegar	1 fresh red chilli, thinly sliced	

1 Trim the stems of the pak choi and shred the leaves.

2 Heat the stock in a large saucepan. Add the pak choi and cook for 10–15 minutes.

3 Mix the rice wine vinegar, soy sauce, sugar and sherry together. Add this mixture to the stock, together with the sliced chilli. Bring to the boil, lower the heat and cook for 2–3 minutes.

4 Blend the cornflour (cornstarch) with the water to form a smooth paste. Gradually stir the cornflour (cornstarch) mixture into the soup. Cook, stirring constantly, until it thickens. Cook for a further 4–5 minutes. Ladle the soup into individual warm serving bowls and serve immediately.

VARIATION

Boil about 2 tbsp rice in lightly salted water until tender. Drain and spoon into the base of the soup bowls. Ladle the soup over the rice and serve immediately.

COOK'S TIP

Pak choi, *also known as bok choi or spoon cabbage, has long, white leaf stalks and fleshy, spoon-shaped, shiny green leaves. There are a number of varieties available, which differ mainly in size rather than flavour.*

Spring Rolls

Serves 4

INGREDIENTS

175 g/6 oz cooked pork, chopped
75 g/2³/4 oz cooked chicken, chopped
1 tsp light soy sauce
1 tsp light brown sugar
1 tsp sesame oil
1 tsp vegetable oil
225 g/8 oz beansprouts

25 g/1 oz canned bamboo shoots, drained, rinsed and chopped
1 green (bell) pepper, seeded and chopped
2 spring onions (scallions), sliced
1 tsp cornflour (cornstarch)
2 tsp water

vegetable oil, for deep-frying

SKINS:
125 g/4¹/2 oz/1¹/8 cups plain (all-purpose) flour
5 tbsp cornflour (cornstarch)
450 ml/16 fl oz/2 cups water
3 tbsp vegetable oil

1 Mix the pork, chicken, soy, sugar and sesame oil. Cover and marinate for 30 minutes. Heat the vegetable oil in a wok. Add the beansprouts, bamboo shoots, (bell) pepper and spring onions (scallions) and stir-fry for 2–3 minutes. Add the meat and the marinade to the wok and stir-fry for 2–3 minutes. Blend the cornflour (cornstarch) with the water and stir the mixture into the wok. Cool.

2 To make the skins, mix the flour and cornflour (cornstarch) and gradually stir in the water, to make a smooth batter. Heat a small, oiled frying pan (skillet). Swirl one-eighth of the batter over the base and cook for 2–3 minutes. Repeat with the remaining batter. Cover with a damp tea towel (dish cloth).

3 Spread out the skins and spoon one-eighth of the filling along the centre of each. Brush the edges with water and fold in the sides, then roll up.

4 Heat the oil for deep-frying in a wok to 180°C/350°F. Cook the spring rolls, in batches, for 2–3 minutes, or until golden and crisp. Remove from the oil with a slotted spoon and drain on absorbent kitchen paper (paper towels). Serve.

Pork Dim Sum

Serves 4

INGREDIENTS

400 g/14 oz minced (ground) pork	50 g/1³/₄ oz canned bamboo shoots, drained, rinsed and chopped	2 tsp sesame oil
2 spring onions (scallions), chopped	1 tbsp light soy sauce	2 tsp caster (superfine) sugar
	1 tbsp dry sherry	1 egg white, lightly beaten
		4¹/₂ tsp cornflour (cornstarch)
		24 wonton wrappers

1 Mix together the minced (ground) pork, spring onions (scallions), bamboo shoots, soy sauce, dry sherry, sesame oil, sugar and beaten egg white in a bowl until well combined.

2 Stir in the cornflour (cornstarch), mixing well to combine.

3 Spread out the wonton wrappers on a work surface (counter). Place a spoonful of the pork and vegetable mixture in the centre of each wonton wrapper and lightly brush the edges of the wrappers with water.

4 Bring the sides of the wrappers together in the centre of the filling, pinching firmly together.

5 Line a steamer with a clean, damp tea towel (dish cloth) and arrange the wontons inside. Cover and steam for 5–7 minutes, until cooked through. Serve.

COOK'S TIP

Bamboo steamers are designed to rest on the sloping sides of a wok above the water. They are available in a range of sizes.

VARIATION

Use prawns (shrimp), minced (ground) chicken or crabmeat for the filling, with other vegetables, such as chopped carrot, and flavourings, such as chilli or ginger, if you prefer.

Crispy Crab Wontons

Serves 4

INGREDIENTS

175 g/6 oz white crabmeat, flaked	1 small fresh red chilli, chopped	1 tsp light soy sauce
50 g/1³/₄ oz canned water chestnuts, drained, rinsed and chopped	1 spring onion (scallion), chopped	¹/₂ tsp lime juice
	1 tbsp cornflour (cornstarch)	24 wonton wrappers
	1 tsp dry sherry	vegetable oil, for deep-frying
		sliced lime, to garnish

1 To make the filling, mix together the crabmeat, water chestnuts, chilli, spring onion (scallion), cornflour (cornstarch), sherry, soy sauce and lime juice.

2 Spread out the wonton wrappers on a work surface (counter) and spoon one portion of the filling into the centre of each wonton wrapper.

3 Dampen the edges of the wonton wrappers with a little water and fold them in half to form triangles. Fold the two pointed ends in towards the centre, moisten with a little water to secure and then pinch together to seal.

4 Heat the oil for deep-frying in a wok or deep-fryer to 180°C–190°C/350°F–375°F, or until a cube of bread browns in 30 seconds. Fry the wontons, in batches, for 2–3 minutes, until golden and crisp. Remove the wontons from the oil and leave to drain on kitchen paper (paper towels).

5 Serve the wontons hot, garnished with slices of lime.

COOK'S TIP

Wonton wrappers, available from Chinese supermarkets, are paper-thin squares made from wheat-flour and egg. They can be easily damaged, so handle them carefully. Make sure that the wontons are sealed well and secured before deep-frying to prevent the filling coming out and the wontons unwrapping.

Pot Sticker Dumplings

Serves 4

INGREDIENTS

DUMPLINGS:
175 g/6 oz/1^1/2 cups plain
    (all-purpose) flour
pinch of salt
3 tbsp vegetable oil
6–8 tbsp boiling water
oil, for deep-frying
125 ml/4 fl oz/^{1}/2 cup water,
    for steaming
sliced spring onions (scallions)
    and chives, to garnish

soy sauce or hoisin sauce, to
    serve

FILLING:
150 g/5^1/2 oz lean chicken,
    very finely chopped
25 g/1 oz canned bamboo
    shoots, drained and
    chopped
2 spring onions (scallions),
    finely chopped

^{1}/2 small red (bell) pepper,
    seeded and finely chopped
^{1}/2 tsp Chinese curry powder
1 tbsp light soy sauce
1 tsp caster (superfine) sugar
1 tsp sesame oil

1 To make the dumplings, mix together the flour and salt in a bowl. Make a well in the centre, add the oil and water and mix well to form a soft dough. Knead the dough on a lightly floured surface, wrap in cling film (plastic wrap) and let stand for 30 minutes.

2 Meanwhile, mix all of the filling ingredients.

3 Divide the dough into 12 equal-sized pieces and roll each piece into a 12.5-cm/5-inch round. Spoon a portion of the filling on to one half of each round. Fold the dough over the filling to form a 'pasty', sealing the edges together.

4 Pour a little oil into a heavy-based frying pan (skillet) and cook the

dumplings, in batches, until browned and crisp. Return all of the dumplings to the pan (skillet) and add about 125 ml/4 fl oz/^{1}/2 cup water. Cover and steam for 5 minutes, or until the dumplings are cooked through. Remove with a slotted spoon and garnish with sliced spring onions (scallions) and chives. Serve with soy or hoisin sauce.

Pancake Rolls

Serves 4

INGREDIENTS
---

4 tsp vegetable oil
1–2 garlic cloves, crushed
225 g/8 oz minced (ground)
   pork
225/8 oz pak choi, shredded

4$\frac{1}{2}$ tsp light soy sauce
$\frac{1}{2}$ tsp sesame oil
8 spring roll skins, 25 cm/
   10 inches square, thawed
   if frozen

oil, for deep-frying
chilli sauce (see Cook's Tip,
   below), to serve

1 Heat the vegetable oil in a preheated wok. Add the garlic and stir-fry for 30 seconds. Add the pork and stir-fry for 2–3 minutes, until just lightly coloured. Add the shredded pak choi, soy sauce and sesame oil to the wok and stir-fry for 2–3 minutes. Remove from the heat and set aside to cool.

2 Spread out the spring roll skins on a work surface (counter) and spoon 2 tbsp of the pork mixture along one edge of each. Roll the skin over

once and fold in the sides. Roll up completely to make a sausage shape, brushing the edges with a little water to seal. If you have time, set the pancake rolls aside for 10 minutes to seal firmly.

3 Heat the oil for deep-frying in a wok until almost smoking. Reduce the heat slightly and fry the pancake rolls, in batches if necessary, for 3–4 minutes, until golden. Remove from the oil with a slotted spoon and drain on kitchen paper (paper towels). Serve with chilli sauce.

COOK'S TIP

To make chilli sauce, heat 60 g/2 oz/¼ cup caster (superfine) sugar, 50 ml/2 fl oz/¼ cup rice vinegar and 2 tbsp water in a small pan, stirring until the sugar has dissolved. Bring the mixture to the boil and boil rapidly until a light syrup forms. Remove the pan from the heat and stir in 2 finely chopped, fresh red chillies. Leave the sauce to cool before serving. If you prefer a milder sauce, deseed the chillies before chopping them.

Sesame Prawn (Shrimp) Toasts

Serves 4

INGREDIENTS

225 g/8 oz cooked, peeled
    prawns (shrimp)
1 spring onion (scallion)
1/4 tsp salt
1 tsp light soy sauce

1 tbsp cornflour (cornstarch)
1 egg white, beaten
3 thin slices white bread,
    crusts removed
4 tbsp sesame seeds

vegetable oil, for deep-frying
chopped chives, to garnish

1 Put the prawns (shrimp) and spring onion (scallion) in a food processor and process until finely minced (ground). Alternatively, chop them very finely. Transfer to a bowl and stir in the salt, soy sauce, cornflour (cornstarch) and egg white.

2 Spread the mixture on to one side of each slice of bread. Spread the sesame seeds on top of the mixture, pressing down well.

3 Cut each slice into 4 equal triangles or strips.

4 Heat the oil for deep-frying in a wok until almost smoking. Carefully place the triangles in the oil, coated side down, and cook for 2–3 minutes, until golden brown. Remove with a slotted spoon and drain on kitchen paper (paper towels). Serve hot.

COOK'S TIP

Fry the triangles in two batches, keeping the first batch warm while you cook the second, to prevent them from overcooking.

VARIATION

If wished, you could add 1/2 tsp very finely chopped fresh root ginger and 1 tsp Chinese rice wine to the prawn (shrimp) mixture at the end of step 1.

Sweet & Sour Battered Prawns (Shrimp)

Serves 4

INGREDIENTS

16 large raw prawns (shrimp),
    peeled
1 tsp grated fresh root ginger
1 garlic clove, crushed
2 spring onions (scallions),
    sliced
2 tbsp dry sherry
2 tsp sesame oil
1 tbsp light soy sauce
vegetable oil, for deep-frying

shredded spring onion
    (scallion), to garnish

BATTER:
4 egg whites
4 tbsp cornflour (cornstarch)
2 tbsp plain (all-purpose) flour

SAUCE:
2 tbsp tomato purée
    (tomato paste)

3 tbsp white wine vinegar
4 tsp light soy sauce
2 tbsp lemon juice
3 tbsp light brown sugar
1 green (bell) pepper, seeded
    and cut into thin
    matchsticks
1/2 tsp chilli sauce
300 ml/1/2 pint/11/4 cups
    vegetable stock
2 tsp cornflour (cornstarch)

1 Using tweezers, devein the prawns (shrimp), then flatten them with a knife.

2 Place the prawns (shrimp) in a dish and add the ginger, garlic, spring onions (scallions), sherry, oil and soy. Cover and marinate for 30 minutes.

3 Make the batter by beating the egg whites until thick. Fold in the cornflour (cornstarch) and flour to form a light batter.

4 Place all of the sauce ingredients in a pan and bring to the boil. Reduce the heat and leave to simmer for 10 minutes.

5 Remove the prawns (shrimp) from the marinade and dip them into the batter to coat.

6 Heat the oil until almost smoking. Reduce the heat and fry the prawns (shrimp) for 3–4 minutes, until crisp. Serve with the sauce.

Prawn (Shrimp) Rice Paper Parcels

Serves 4

INGREDIENTS

1 egg white
2 tsp cornflour (cornstarch)
2 tsp dry sherry
1 tsp caster (superfine) sugar
2 tsp hoisin sauce
225 g/8 oz peeled, cooked
    prawns (shrimp)

4 spring onions (scallions),
    sliced
25 g/1 oz canned water
    chestnuts, drained, rinsed
    and chopped

8 Chinese rice paper wrappers
vegetable oil, for deep-frying
hoisin sauce or plum sauce,
    to serve

1 Lightly beat the egg white, then mix in the cornflour (cornstarch), dry sherry, sugar and hoisin sauce. Add the prawns (shrimp), spring onions (scallions) and water chestnuts, mixing well.

2 Soften the rice papers by dipping them in a bowl of water one at a time. Spread them out on a work surface (counter).

3 Spoon a little of the prawn (shrimp)

mixture into the centre of each rice paper and wrap the paper around the filling to make a secure parcel.

4 Heat the oil in a wok until it is almost smoking. Reduce the heat slightly, add the parcels, in batches, and deep-fry for 4–5 minutes, until crisp. Remove from the oil with a slotted spoon and drain on kitchen paper (paper towels).

5 Transfer the parcels to a warmed serving dish

and serve immediately with a little hoisin or plum sauce.

COOK'S TIP

*Use this filling inside
wonton wrappers if the
rice paper wrappers
are unavailable.*

Crab Ravioli

Serves 4

INGREDIENTS

450 g/1 lb crabmeat (fresh or canned and drained)	25 g/1 oz beansprouts, roughly chopped	1 small egg, beaten
1/2 red (bell) pepper, seeded and finely diced	1 tbsp light soy sauce	2 tbsp peanut oil
125 g/4¹/2 oz Chinese leaves (cabbage), shredded	1 tsp lime juice	1 tsp sesame oil
	16 wonton wrappers	salt and pepper

1 Mix together the crabmeat, (bell) pepper, Chinese leaves (cabbage), beansprouts, soy sauce and lime juice in a bowl. Season and leave to stand for 15 minutes, stirring occasionally.

2 Spread out the wonton wrappers on a work surface (counter). Spoon a little of the crabmeat mixture into the centre of each wrapper, dividing it equally between them. Reserve the remaining crabmeat filling.

3 Brush the edges of the wrappers with the beaten egg and fold in half, pushing out any air. Press the edges together with your fingers to seal tightly.

4 Heat the peanut oil in a preheated wok or frying pan (skillet). Fry the ravioli, in batches, for 3–4 minutes, turning until browned. Remove with a slotted spoon and drain on paper towels.

5 Heat the remaining filling in the wok or frying pan (skillet) over a gentle heat until hot. Serve the ravioli with the hot filling and sprinkled with sesame oil.

COOK'S TIP

Make sure that the edges of the ravioli are sealed well and that all of the air is pressed out to prevent them from opening during cooking.

Spare Ribs

Serves 4

INGREDIENTS

900 g/2 lb pork spare ribs	pinch of Chinese five spice	coriander (cilantro) sprigs, to
2 tbsp dark soy sauce	powder	garnish (optional)
3 tbsp hoisin sauce	2 tsp dark brown sugar	
1 tbsp Chinese rice wine or dry	1/4 tsp chilli sauce	
sherry	2 garlic cloves, crushed	

1 Cut the spare ribs into separate pieces if they are joined together. If desired, you can chop them into 5 cm/2-inch lengths, using a cleaver.

2 Mix together the soy sauce, hoisin sauce, Chinese rice wine or sherry, Chinese five spice powder, dark brown sugar, chilli sauce and garlic.

3 Place the ribs in a shallow dish and pour the mixture over them, turning to coat them well. Cover and marinate in the refrigerator, turning the ribs from time to time, for at least 1 hour.

4 Remove the ribs from the marinade and arrange them in a single layer on a wire rack placed over a roasting tin (pan) half filled with warm water. Brush with the marinade, reserving the remainder.

5 Cook in a preheated oven, at 180°C/350°F/ Gas Mark 4, for 30 minutes. Remove the roasting tin (pan) from the oven and turn the ribs over.

Brush with the remaining marinade and return to the oven for a further 30 minutes, or until cooked through. Transfer to a warmed serving dish, garnish with the coriander (cilantro) sprigs (if using) and serve immediately.

COOK'S TIP

Add more hot water to the roasting tin (pan) during cooking if required. Do not allow it to dry out as the water steams the ribs and aids in their cooking.

Honeyed Chicken Wings

Serves 4

INGREDIENTS

450 g/1 lb chicken wings
2 tbsp peanut oil
2 tbsp light soy sauce
2 tbsp hoisin sauce
2 tbsp clear honey
2 garlic cloves, crushed
1 tsp sesame seeds

MARINADE:
1 dried red chilli
1/2–1 tsp chilli powder
1/2–1 tsp ground ginger
finely grated rind of 1 lime

1 To make the marinade, crush the dried chilli in a pestle and mortar. Mix together the crushed dried chilli, chilli powder, ground ginger and lime rind in a small bowl.

2 Rub the spice mixture into the chicken wings with your fingertips. Set aside for at least 2 hours to allow the flavours to penetrate the chicken wings.

3 Heat the peanut oil in a preheated wok.

4 Add the chicken wings to the wok and fry, turning frequently, for 10–12 minutes, until golden and crisp. Drain off any excess oil.

5 Add the soy sauce, hoisin sauce, honey, garlic and sesame seeds to the wok, turning the chicken wings to coat them with the mixture.

6 Reduce the heat and cook for 20–25 minutes, turning the

chicken wings frequently, until completely cooked through. Serve hot.

COOK'S TIP

Make the dish in advance and freeze the chicken wings. Defrost thoroughly, cover with foil and heat right through in a moderate oven.

Steamed Duck Dumplings

Serves 4

INGREDIENTS

DUMPLING DOUGH:
300 g/10^1/$_2$ oz/2^2/$_3$ cups plain
 (all-purpose) flour
15 g/^{1}/$_2$ oz dried yeast
1 tsp caster (superfine) sugar
2 tbsp warm water
175 ml/6 fl oz/^{3}/$_4$ cup warm
 milk

FILLING:
300 g/10^1/$_2$ oz duck breast
1 tbsp light brown sugar
1 tbsp light soy sauce
2 tbsp clear honey
1 tbsp hoisin sauce
1 tbsp vegetable oil
1 leek, finely chopped

1 garlic clove, crushed
1-cm/^{1}/$_2$-inch piece fresh root
 ginger (ginger root), grated

---

1 To make the filling, place the duck breast in a bowl. Mix the sugar, soy sauce, honey and hoisin sauce. Pour the mixture over the duck and marinate for 20 minutes. Remove the duck from the marinade and cook on a rack set over a roasting tin (pan) in a preheated oven, at 200°C/400°F/Gas Mark 6, for 35–40 minutes, or until cooked through. Let cool, remove the meat from the bones and cut into small cubes.

2 Heat the oil in a wok and fry the leek, garlic and ginger for 3 minutes. Mix with the duck meat.

3 To make the dough, sift the flour into a bowl. Mix the yeast, sugar and water in a separate bowl and leave in a warm place for 15 minutes. Pour the yeast mixture into the flour, with the warm milk, mixing to form a firm dough. Knead the dough on a floured surface for 5 minutes. Roll into a sausage shape, 2.5 cm/1 inch in diameter. Cut into 16 pieces, cover and let stand for 20–25 minutes. Flatten the pieces into 10-cm/4-inch rounds. Place a spoonful of filling in the centre of each, draw up the sides to form a 'moneybag' shape and twist to seal.

4 Place the dumplings on a clean, damp tea towel (dish cloth) in the base of a steamer, cover and steam for 20 minutes.

Spinach Meatballs

Serves 4

INGREDIENTS

125 g/4¹/2 oz pork
1 small egg
1-cm/¹/2-inch piece fresh root
    ginger (ginger root),
    chopped
1 small onion, finely chopped
1 tbsp boiling water

25 g/1 oz canned bamboo
    shoots, drained, rinsed and
    chopped
2 slices smoked ham, chopped
2 tsp cornflour (cornstarch)
450 g/1 lb fresh spinach
2 tsp sesame seeds

SAUCE:
150 ml/¹/4 pint/²/3 cup
    vegetable stock
¹/2 tsp cornflour (cornstarch)
1 tsp cold water
1 tsp light soy sauce
¹/2 tsp sesame oil
1 tbsp chopped chives

1 Mince (grind) the pork very finely in a food processor or meat mincer (grinder). Lightly beat the egg in a bowl and stir into the pork.

2 Put the ginger and onion in a separate bowl, add the boiling water and let stand for 5 minutes. Drain and add to the pork mixture with the bamboo shoots, ham and cornflour (cornstarch). Mix well and roll into 12 balls.

3 Wash the spinach and remove the stalks. Blanch in boiling water for 10 seconds and drain well, pressing out as much moisture as possible. Slice the spinach into very thin strips, then mix with the sesame seeds. Spread out the mixture in a shallow baking tin (pan). Roll the meatballs in the mixture to coat.

4 Place the meatballs on a heatproof plate in the base of a steamer. Cover and steam for 8–10 minutes, until cooked through and tender.

5 Meanwhile, make the sauce. Put the stock in a saucepan and bring to the boil. Mix together the cornflour (cornstarch) and water to a smooth paste and stir it into the stock. Stir in the soy sauce, sesame oil and chives. Transfer the cooked meatballs to a warm plate and serve with the sauce.

Steamed Cabbage Rolls

Serves 4

INGREDIENTS

8 cabbage leaves, trimmed	1 tsp cornflour (cornstarch)	1 garlic clove, thinly sliced
225 g/8 oz skinless, boneless	$\frac{1}{2}$ tsp chilli powder	sliced fresh red chilli, to
chicken	1 egg lightly beaten	garnish
175 g/6 oz peeled raw or	1 tbsp vegetable oil	
cooked prawns (shrimp)	1 leek, sliced	

1 Bring a large saucepan of water to the boil. Blanch the cabbage leaves for 2 minutes. Drain, rinse under cold water and drain again. Pat dry with kitchen paper (paper towels) and spread out on a work surface (counter).

2 Put the chicken and prawns (shrimp) into a food processor and process until finely minced (ground). Alternatively, mince (grind) in a meat mincer (grinder). Transfer to a bowl and add the cornflour (cornstarch),

chilli powder and egg, mixing together well.

3 Place 2 tablespoons of the chicken and prawn (shrimp) mixture towards one end of each cabbage leaf. Fold the sides of the cabbage leaf around the filling and roll up to form a firm parcel.

4 Arrange the cabbage parcels, seam-side down, in a single layer on a heatproof plate and cook in a steamer for 10 minutes, or until cooked through.

5 Heat the vegetable oil in a preheated wok. Add the leek and garlic and sauté for 1–2 minutes.

6 Transfer the cabbage parcels to warmed individual serving plates and garnish with red chilli slices. Serve with the leek and garlic sauté.

COOK'S TIP

Use Chinese cabbage or Savoy cabbage for this recipe, choosing leaves of a similar size for the parcels.

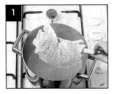

Chinese Omelette

Serves 4

INGREDIENTS

8 eggs	2 tbsp chopped chives
225 g/8 oz/2 cups cooked chicken, shredded	2 tsp light soy sauce
12 tiger prawns (jumbo shrimp), peeled and deveined	dash of chilli sauce
	2 tbsp vegetable oil

1 Lightly beat the eggs in a large mixing bowl.

2 Add the shredded chicken and tiger prawns (jumbo shrimp) to the eggs, mixing well.

3 Stir in the chopped chives, soy sauce and chilli sauce, mixing well.

4 Heat the oil in a large frying pan (skillet) over a medium heat and add the egg mixture, tilting the pan to coat the base completely. Cook over a medium heat, gently stirring the omelette with a fork, until the surface is just set and the underside is a golden brown colour.

5 When the omelette is set, slide it out of the pan, with the aid of a palette knife (spatula).

6 Cut the omelette into squares or slices to serve.

VARIATION

You could add extra flavour to the omelette by stirring in 3 tbsp finely chopped fresh coriander (cilantro) or 1 tsp sesame seeds with the chives in step 3.

COOK'S TIP

Add peas or other vegetables to the omelette and serve as a main course for 2 people.

Main Courses

This comprehensive chapter covers many cooking methods and ingredients to give a very wide variety of main meals for all occasions, be it a simple supper, a dinner party or informal gathering. Fish, seafood, pork, lamb, beef, duck and chicken are all used to their full potential to delight the palate.

When choosing ingredients, try to purchase them as fresh as possible, particularly fish and seafood. You can vary the meat and fish used to suit your personal preference, as they are very adaptable recipes.

When entertaining, choose several different dishes to give as much variety of taste as possible, and prepare as much as you can in advance to enable you to spend more time with your guests than in the kitchen.

The portions in the recipes contained in this chapter are geared towards the traditional Chinese menu, and may be slightly smaller than a Western serving, so why not choose a selection and create your very own Chinese banquet!

Steamed Fish with Black Bean Sauce

Serves 4

INGREDIENTS

900 g/2 lb whole snapper,
   cleaned and scaled
3 garlic cloves, crushed
2 tbsp black bean sauce
1 tsp cornflour (cornstarch)

2 tsp sesame oil
2 tbsp light soy sauce
2 tsp caster (superfine) sugar
2 tbsp dry sherry
1 small leek, shredded

1 small red (bell) pepper,
   seeded and cut into thin
   strips
shredded leek and lemon
   wedges, to garnish
boiled rice or noodles, to serve

1 Rinse the fish inside and out with cold running water and pat dry with kitchen paper (paper towels). Make 2-3 diagonal slashes in the flesh on each side of the fish, using a sharp knife. Rub the garlic into the fish.

2 Thoroughly mix the black bean sauce, cornflour (cornstarch), sesame oil, light soy sauce, sugar and dry sherry together in a bowl. Place the fish in a shallow heatproof dish and pour the sauce mixture over the top.

3 Sprinkle the leek and (bell) pepper strips on top of the sauce. Place the dish in the top of a steamer, cover and steam for 10 minutes, or until the fish is cooked through.

4 Transfer to a serving dish, garnish with shredded leek and lemon wedges and serve with boiled rice or noodles.

VARIATION

Whole sea bream or sea bass may be used in this recipe instead of snapper, if you prefer.

COOK'S TIP

Insert the point of a sharp knife into the fish to test if it is cooked. The fish is cooked through if the knife goes into the flesh easily.

Steamed Snapper with Fruit & Ginger Stuffing

Serves 4

INGREDIENTS

1.4 kg/3 lb whole snapper, cleaned and scaled
175 g/6 oz spinach
orange slices and shredded spring onions (scallions), to garnish

STUFFING:
60 g/2 oz/2 cups cooked long-grain rice
1 tsp grated fresh root ginger
2 spring onions (scallions), finely chopped

2 tsp light soy sauce
1 tsp sesame oil
1/2 tsp ground star anise
1 orange, segmented and chopped

1 Rinse the fish inside and out under cold running water and pat dry with kitchen paper (paper towels). Blanch the spinach for 40 seconds, rinse in cold water and drain well, pressing out as much moisture as possible. Arrange the spinach on a heatproof plate and place the fish on top.

2 To make the stuffing, mix together the cooked rice, grated ginger, spring onion (scallion), soy sauce, sesame oil, star anise and orange in a bowl.

3 Spoon the stuffing into the body cavity of the fish, pressing it in well with a spoon.

4 Cover the plate and cook in a steamer for 10 minutes, or until the fish is cooked through. Transfer the fish to a warmed serving dish, garnish with orange slices and shredded spring onion (scallion) and serve immediately.

COOK'S TIP

The name snapper covers a family of tropical and subtropical fish that vary in colour. They may be red, orange, pink, red, grey or blue-green. Some are striped or spotted and they range in size from about 15 cm/ 6 inches to 90 cm/3 ft.

Trout with Pineapple

Serves 4

INGREDIENTS
---

4 trout fillets, skinned
2 tbsp vegetable oil
2 garlic cloves, cut into slivers
4 slices fresh pineapple, peeled
   and diced
1 celery stick, sliced
1 tbsp light soy sauce

50 ml/2 fl oz/^{1}/4 cup fresh or
   unsweetened pineapple
   juice
150 ml/^{1}/4 pint/^{2}/3 cup fish
   stock
1 tsp cornflour (cornstarch)
2 tsp water

shredded celery leaves and
   fresh red chilli strips, to
   garnish

1 Cut the trout fillets into strips. Heat 1 tbsp of the oil in a preheated wok until almost smoking. Reduce the heat slightly, add the fish and sauté for 2 minutes. Remove from the wok and set aside.

2 Add the remaining oil to the wok, reduce the heat and add the garlic, pineapple and celery. Stir-fry for 1–2 minutes.

3 Add the soy sauce, pineapple juice and fish stock to the wok. Bring to the boil and cook, stirring, for 2–3 minutes, or until the sauce has reduced.

4 Blend the cornflour (cornstarch) with the water to form a paste and stir it into the wok. Bring the sauce to the boil and cook, stirring constantly, until the sauce thickens and clears.

5 Return the fish to the wok, and cook, stirring gently, until heated through. Transfer to a warmed serving dish and serve, garnished with shredded celery leaves and red chilli strips.

COOK'S TIP

Use canned pineapple instead of fresh pineapple if you wish, choosing slices in unsweetened, natural juice in preference to a syrup.

Mullet with Ginger

Serves 4

INGREDIENTS

1 whole mullet, cleaned and
    scaled
2 spring onions (scallions),
    chopped
1 tsp grated fresh root ginger
125 ml/4 fl oz/$^1/_2$ cup garlic
    wine vinegar

125 ml/4 fl oz/$^1/_2$ cup light
    soy sauce
3 tsp caster (superfine) sugar
dash of chilli sauce
125 ml/4 fl oz/$^1/_2$ cup fish
    stock
1 green (bell) pepper, seeded
    and thinly sliced

1 large tomato, skinned,
    seeded and cut into thin
    strips
salt and pepper
sliced tomato, to garnish

1 Rinse the fish inside and out and pat dry with kitchen paper (paper towels).

2 Make 3 diagonal slits in the flesh on each side of the fish. Season with salt and pepper inside and out.

3 Place the fish on a heatproof plate and scatter the spring onions (scallions) and ginger over the top. Cover and steam

for 10 minutes, or until the fish is cooked through.

4 Place the vinegar, soy sauce, sugar, chilli sauce, fish stock, (bell) pepper and tomato in a saucepan and bring to the boil, stirring occasionally. Cook over a high heat until the sauce has slightly reduced and thickened.

5 Remove the fish from the steamer and transfer to a warm serving

dish. Pour the sauce over the fish, garnish with tomato slices and serve immediately.

COOK'S TIP

Use fillets of fish for this recipe if preferred, and reduce the cooking time to 5–7 minutes.

Szechuan White Fish

Serves 4

INGREDIENTS

350 g/12 oz white fish fillets	1 onion, finely chopped	175 ml/6 fl oz/³/4 cup fish
1 small egg, beaten	1 celery stick, chopped	stock
3 tbsp plain (all-purpose) flour	1 fresh red chilli, chopped	1 tsp caster (superfine) sugar
4 tbsp dry white wine	3 spring onions (scallions),	1 tsp cornflour (cornstarch)
3 tbsp light soy sauce	chopped	2 tsp water
vegetable oil, for frying	1 tsp rice wine vinegar	chilli flowers and celery leaves,
1 garlic clove, cut into slivers	¹/2 tsp ground Szechuan	to garnish (optional)
1-cm/¹/2-inch piece fresh root	pepper	
ginger, finely chopped		

1 Cut the fish into 4-cm/ 1½-inch cubes.

2 In a bowl, beat the egg, flour, wine and 1 tbsp of soy sauce to make a batter.

3 Dip the cubes of fish into the batter to coat.

4 Heat the oil in a preheated wok until it is almost smoking. Reduce the heat slightly and cook the fish, in batches, for 2–3 minutes, until golden. Drain on kitchen paper (paper towels) and set aside.

5 Pour all but 1 tbsp of oil from the wok and return to the heat. Add the garlic, ginger, onion, celery, chilli and spring onions (scallions) and stir-fry for 1–2 minutes.

6 Stir in the remaining soy sauce and the vinegar.

7 Add the Szechuan pepper, fish stock and sugar to the wok. Blend the cornflour (cornstarch) with the water to form a smooth paste and stir it into the stock. Bring to the boil and cook, stirring, for 1 minute, until the sauce thickens and clears.

8 Return the fish to the wok and cook for 1–2 minutes, until hot. Transfer to a serving dish.

Crispy Fish

Serves 4

INGREDIENTS

450 g/1 lb white fish fillets	4 tbsp milk	3 tbsp tomato purée (paste)
	vegetable oil, for deep-frying	1 tbsp rice wine vinegar
BATTER:		2 tbsp dark soy sauce
60 g/2 oz/$^1/_2$ cup plain	SAUCE:	2 tbsp Chinese rice wine
(all-purpose) flour	1 fresh red chilli, chopped	2 tbsp water
1 egg, separated	2 garlic cloves, crushed	pinch of caster (superfine)
1 tbsp peanut oil	pinch of chilli powder	sugar

1 Cut the fish into 2.5-cm/1-inch cubes and set aside. To make the batter, sift the flour into a bowl and make a well in the centre. Add the egg yolk and oil to the bowl and stir in the milk, incorporating the flour to form a smooth batter. Let stand for 20 minutes.

2 Whisk the egg white until it forms peaks and fold it into the batter. Heat the oil in a preheated wok. Dip the fish into the batter and fry, in batches, for 8–10 minutes, until cooked through..Remove the fish from the wok with a slotted spoon, set aside and keep warm.

3 Pour off all but 1 tbsp of oil from the wok and return to the heat. To make the sauce, add the chilli, garlic, chilli powder, tomato purée (paste), rice wine vinegar, soy sauce, Chinese rice wine, water and sugar and cook, stirring, for 3–4 minutes.

4 Return the fish to the wok and stir gently to coat it in the sauce. Cook for 2-3 minutes, until hot. Transfer the fish and sauce to a serving dish and serve immediately.

COOK'S TIP

Take care when pouring hot oil from the wok and ensure that you transfer it to a suitable bowl until cool.

Seafood Medley

Serves 4

INGREDIENTS

2 tbsp dry white wine
1 egg white, lightly beaten
$^1/_2$ tsp Chinese five spice powder
1 tsp cornflour (cornstarch)
300 g/10$^1/_2$ oz raw prawns (shrimp), peeled and deveined

125 g/4$^1/_2$ oz prepared squid, cut into rings
125 g/4$^1/_2$ oz white fish fillets, cut into strips
vegetable oil, for deep-frying
1 green (bell) pepper, seeded and cut into thin strips
1 carrot, cut into thin strips

4 baby corn cobs, halved lengthways

1 Mix together the wine, egg white, Chinese five spice powder and cornflour (cornstarch) in a large bowl. Add the prawns (shrimp), squid rings and fish fillets and stir to coat evenly. Remove the fish and seafood with a slotted spoon, reserving any leftover cornflour (cornstarch) mixture.

2 Heat the oil in a preheated wok and deep-fry the prawns (shrimp), squid and fish for 2–3 minutes. Remove the seafood mixture from the wok with a slotted spoon and set aside.

3 Pour off all but 1 tablespoon of oil from the wok and return to the heat. Add the (bell) pepper, carrot and corn cobs and stir-fry for 4–5 minutes.

4 Return the seafood mixture to the wok and add any remaining cornflour mixture. Cook, stirring and tossing well, to heat through. Transfer to a serving plate and serve immediately.

COOK'S TIP

Open up the squid rings and using a sharp knife, score a lattice pattern on the flesh to make them look more attractive.

Fried Prawns (Shrimp) with Cashews

Serves 4

INGREDIENTS

2 garlic cloves, crushed
1 tbsp cornflour (cornstarch)
pinch of caster (superfine)
 sugar
450 g/1 lb raw tiger prawns
 (jumbo shrimp)
4 tbsp vegetable oil

1 leek, sliced
125 g/4^{1}/$_{2}$ oz broccoli florets
1 orange (bell) pepper, seeded
 and diced
75 g/2^{3}/$_{4}$ oz/^{3}/$_{4}$ cup unsalted
 cashew nuts

SAUCE:
175 ml/6 fl oz/^{3}/$_{4}$ cup fish
 stock
1 tbsp cornflour (cornstarch)
dash of chilli sauce
2 tsp sesame oil
1 tbsp Chinese rice wine

1 Mix together the garlic, cornflour (cornstarch) and sugar in a bowl. Peel and devein the prawns (shrimp). Stir the prawns (shrimp) into the mixture to coat.

2 Heat the oil in a preheated wok and add the prawn (shrimp) mixture. Stir-fry over a high heat for 20–30 seconds until the prawns (shrimp) turn pink. Remove the prawns (shrimp) from the wok

with a slotted spoon and set aside.

3 Add the leek, broccoli and (bell) pepper to the wok and stir-fry for 2 minutes.

4 To make the sauce, mix together the fish stock, cornflour (cornstarch), chilli sauce to taste, the sesame oil and Chinese rice wine. Add the mixture to the wok, together with the cashew nuts. Return the prawns (shrimp) to the

wok and cook for 1 minute to heat through. Transfer to a warm serving dish and serve immediately.

VARIATION

This recipe also works well with chicken, pork or beef strips instead of the prawns (shrimp). Use 225 g/8 oz meat instead of 450 g/1 lb prawns (shrimp).

(Small) Shrimp Fu Yong

Serves 4

INGREDIENTS

2 tbsp vegetable oil
1 carrot, grated
5 eggs, beaten
225 g/8 oz raw (small) shrimp,
   peeled

1 tbsp light soy sauce
pinch of Chinese five spice
   powder
2 spring onions (scallions),
   chopped

2 tsp sesame seeds
1 tsp sesame oil

1 Heat the vegetable oil in a preheated wok.

2 Add the carrot and stir-fry for 1–2 minutes.

3 Push the carrot to one side of the wok and add the eggs. Cook, stirring gently, for 1–2 minutes.

4 Stir the (small) shrimp, soy sauce and five spice powder into the mixture in the wok. Stir-fry the mixture for 2–3 minutes, or until the (small) shrimps change colour and the mixture is almost dry.

5 Turn the (small) shrimp fu yong out on to a warm plate and sprinkle the spring onions (scallions), sesame seeds and sesame oil on top. Serve immediately.

VARIATION

For a more substantial dish, you could add 225 g/8 oz/ 1 cup cooked long-grain rice with the (small) shrimp in step 4. Taste and adjust the quantities of soy sauce, Chinese five spice powder and sesame oil if necessary.

COOK'S TIP

If only cooked prawns (shrimp) are available, add them just before the end of cooking, but make sure that they are fully incorporated into the fu yong. They require only heating through – overcooking will make them chewy and tasteless.

Cantonese Prawns (Shrimp)

Serves 4

INGREDIENTS

5 tbsp vegetable oil
4 garlic cloves, crushed
675 g/1¹/₂ lb raw prawns
  (shrimp), shelled and
  deveined
5-cm/2-inch piece fresh root
  ginger, chopped
175 g/6 oz lean pork, diced

1 leek, sliced
3 eggs, beaten
shredded leek and red (bell)
  pepper matchsticks, to
  garnish

SAUCE:
2 tbsp dry sherry
2 tbsp light soy sauce
2 tsp caster (superfine) sugar
150 ml/¹/₄ pint/²/₃ cup fish
  stock
4¹/₂ tsp cornflour (cornstarch)
3 tbsp water

1 Heat 2 tablespoons of the oil in a preheated wok. Add the garlic and stir-fry for 30 seconds. Add the prawns (shrimp) and stir-fry for 5 minutes, or until they change colour. Remove the prawns (shrimp) from the wok with a slotted spoon, set aside and keep warm.

2 Add the remaining oil to the wok and heat. Add the ginger, diced pork and leek and stir-fry over a medium heat for 4–5 minutes, or until the pork is lightly coloured.

3 Add the sherry, soy, sugar and fish stock to the wok. Blend the cornflour (cornstarch) with the water to form a smooth paste and stir it into the wok. Cook, stirring, until the sauce thickens and clears.

4 Return the prawns (shrimp) to the wok and add the beaten eggs. Cook for 5–6 minutes, gently stirring occasionally, until the eggs set. Transfer to a warm serving dish, garnish with shredded leek and (bell) pepper matchsticks and serve immediately.

COOK'S TIP

If possible, use Chinese rice wine instead of the sherry.

Squid With Oyster Sauce

Serves 4

INGREDIENTS

450 g/1 lb squid	60 g/2 oz mangetout (snow	SAUCE:
150 ml/^{1}/$_4$ pint/^{2}/$_3$ cup	peas)	1 tbsp oyster sauce
vegetable oil	5 tbsp hot fish stock	1 tbsp light soy sauce
1-cm/^{1}/$_2$-inch piece fresh root	red (bell) pepper triangles, to	pinch of caster (superfine)
ginger, grated	garnish	sugar
		1 garlic clove, crushed

1 To prepare the squid, cut down the centre of the body lengthways. Flatten the squid out, inside uppermost, and score a lattice design deep into the flesh, using a sharp knife.

2 To make the sauce, combine the oyster sauce, soy sauce, sugar and garlic in a small bowl. Stir to dissolve the sugar and set aside until required.

3 Heat the oil in a preheated wok until almost smoking. Lower the heat slightly, add the squid and stir-fry until they curl up. Remove with a slotted spoon and drain thoroughly on kitchen paper (paper towels).

4 Pour off all but 2 tablespoons of the oil and return the wok to the heat. Add the ginger and mangetout (snow peas) and stir-fry for 1 minute.

5 Return the squid to the wok and pour in the sauce and hot fish stock. Leave the mixture to simmer for 3 minutes, or until thickened.

6 Transfer to a warm serving dish, garnish with (bell) pepper triangles and serve immediately.

COOK'S TIP

Take care not to overcook the squid, otherwise it will be rubbery and unappetizing.

Scallops in Ginger Sauce

Serves 4

INGREDIENTS

2 tbsp vegetable oil
450 g/1 lb scallops, cleaned
and halved
2.5-cm/1-inch piece fresh root
ginger, finely chopped
3 garlic cloves, crushed

2 leeks, shredded
75 g/2³/4 oz/³/4 cup shelled
peas
125 g/4¹/2 oz canned bamboo
shoots, drained and rinsed
2 tbsp light soy sauce

2 tbsp unsweetened orange
juice
1 tsp caster (superfine) sugar
orange zest, to garnish

1 Heat the oil in a wok. Add the scallops and stir-fry for 1–2 minutes. Remove the scallops from the wok with a slotted spoon and set aside.

2 Add the ginger and garlic to the wok and stir-fry for 30 seconds. Stir in the leeks and peas and cook, stirring, for 2 minutes.

3 Add the bamboo shoots and return the scallops to the wok. Stir gently to mix without breaking up the scallops.

4 Stir in the soy sauce, orange juice and sugar and cook for 1–2 minutes. Transfer to a serving dish, garnish and serve.

COOK'S TIP

The edible parts of a scallop are the round white muscle and the orange and white coral or roe. The frilly skirt surrounding the muscle – the gills and mantle – may be used for making shellfish stock. All other parts should be discarded.

COOK'S TIP

Frozen scallops may be thawed and used in this recipe, adding them at the end of cooking to prevent them from breaking up. If you are buying scallops already shelled, check whether they are fresh or frozen. Fresh scallops are cream coloured and more translucent, while frozen scallops tend to be pure white.

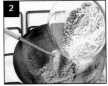

Crab in Ginger Sauce

Serves 4

INGREDIENTS

2 small cooked crabs
2 tbsp vegetable oil
9-cm/3-inch piece fresh root
   ginger, grated
2 garlic cloves, thinly sliced

1 green (bell) pepper, seeded
   and cut into thin strips
6 spring onions (scallions), cut
   into 2.5-cm/1-inch lengths
2 tbsp dry sherry

$^1/_2$ tsp sesame oil
150 ml/$^1/_4$ pint/$^2/_3$ cup fish
   stock
1 tsp light brown sugar
2 tsp cornflour (cornstarch)
150 ml/$^1/_4$ pint/$^2/_3$ cup water

1 Rinse the crabs and gently loosen around the shell at the top. Using a sharp knife, cut away the grey tissue and discard. Rinse the crabs again.

2 Twist off the legs and claws from the crabs. Using a pair of crab claw crackers or a cleaver, crack the claws to break through the shell to expose the flesh. Remove and discard any loose pieces of shell.

3 Separate the body and discard the inedible

lungs and sac. Cut down the centre of each crab to separate the body into two pieces and then cut each of these in half again.

4 Heat the oil in a preheated wok. Add the ginger and garlic and stir-fry for 1 minute. Add the crab pieces and stir-fry for 1 minute.

5 Stir in the (bell) pepper, spring onions (scallions), sherry, sesame oil, stock and sugar. Bring to the boil, reduce the heat,

cover and simmer for 3–4 minutes.

6 Blend the cornflour (cornstarch) with the remaining water and stir it into the wok. Bring to the boil, stirring, until the sauce is thickened and clear. Serve.

COOK'S TIP

If preferred, remove the crabmeat from the shells prior to stir-frying and add to the wok with the (bell) pepper.

Chilli Chicken

Serves 4

INGREDIENTS

350 g/12 oz skinless, boneless
    lean chicken
$^{1}/_{2}$ tsp salt
1 egg white, lightly beaten
2 tbsp cornflour (cornstarch)
4 tbsp vegetable oil
2 garlic cloves, crushed

1-cm/$^{1}/_{2}$-inch piece fresh root
    ginger, grated
1 red (bell) pepper, seeded and
    diced
1 green (bell) pepper, seeded
    and diced
2 fresh red chillies, chopped

2 tbsp light soy sauce
1 tbsp dry sherry or Chinese
    rice wine
1 tbsp wine vinegar

1 Cut the chicken into cubes and place in a mixing bowl. Add the salt, egg white, cornflour (cornstarch) and 1 tbsp of the oil. Turn the chicken in the mixture to coat well.

2 Heat the remaining oil in a preheated wok. Add the garlic and ginger and stir-fry for 30 seconds.

3 Add the chicken pieces to the wok and stir-fry for 2–3 minutes, or until browned.

4 Stir in the (bell) peppers, chillies, soy sauce, sherry or Chinese rice wine and wine vinegar and cook for 2–3 minutes, until the chicken is cooked through. Transfer to a serving dish and serve.

VARIATION

This recipe works well if you use 350 g/12 oz lean steak, cut into thin strips or 450 g/ 1 lb raw prawns (shrimp) instead of the chicken.

COOK'S TIP

When preparing chillies, wear rubber gloves to prevent the juices from burning and irritating your hands. Be careful not to touch your face, especially your lips or eyes, until you have washed your hands.

Lemon Chicken

Serves 4

INGREDIENTS

vegetable oil, for deep-frying
650 g/1 1/2 lb skinless, boneless
   chicken, cut into strips
lemon slices and shredded
   spring onions (scallions),
   to garnish

SAUCE:
1 tbsp cornflour (cornstarch)
6 tbsp cold water
3 tbsp fresh lemon juice
2 tbsp sweet sherry
1/2 tsp caster (superfine) sugar

1 Heat the oil in a wok until almost smoking. Reduce the heat and stir-fry the chicken strips for 3–4 minutes, until cooked through. Remove the chicken with a slotted spoon, set aside and keep warm. Drain the oil from the wok.

2 To make the sauce, mix the cornflour with 2 tablespoons of the water to form a paste.

3 Pour the lemon juice and remaining water into the mixture in the wok. Add the sherry and sugar and bring to the boil, stirring until the sugar has completely dissolved.

4 Stir in the cornflour mixture and return to the boil. Reduce the heat and simmer, stirring constantly, for 2-3 minutes, until the sauce is thickened and clear.

5 Transfer the chicken to a warm serving plate and pour the sauce over the top. Garnish with the lemon slices and shredded spring onions (scallions) and serve immediately.

COOK'S TIP

If you would prefer to use chicken portions rather than strips, cook them in the oil, covered, over a low heat for about 30 minutes, or until cooked through.

Braised Chicken

Serves 4

INGREDIENTS

1.5 kg/3 lb 5 oz chicken
3 tbsp vegetable oil
1 tbsp peanut oil
2 tbsp dark brown sugar
5 tbsp dark soy sauce

150 ml/$^{1}/_{4}$ pint/$^{2}/_{3}$ cup water
2 garlic cloves, crushed
1 small onion, chopped
1 fresh red chilli, chopped

celery leaves and chives, to garnish

1 Clean the chicken with damp kitchen paper (paper towels).

2 Put the oil in a wok, add the sugar and heat gently until the sugar caramelizes. Stir in the soy sauce. Add the chicken and turn it in the mixture to coat on all sides.

3 Add the water, garlic, onion and chilli. Cover and simmer, turning the chicken occasionally, for 1 hour, or until cooked through. Test by piercing a thigh with the point of a knife or a skewer – the juices will run clear when the chicken is cooked.

4 Remove the chicken from the wok and transfer to a serving plate. Increase the heat and reduce the sauce in the wok until thickened. Garnish the chicken and serve with the sauce.

COOK'S TIP

When caramelizing the sugar, do not turn the heat too high, or it may burn.

VARIATION

For a spicier sauce, add 1 tbsp finely chopped fresh root ginger and 1 tbsp ground Szechuan peppercorns with the chilli in step 3. If the flavour of dark soy sauce is too strong for your taste, substitute 2 tbsp dark soy sauce and 3 tbsp light soy sauce. This will result in a more delicate taste without sacrificing the attractive colour of the dish.

Chicken With Cashew Nuts & Vegetables

Serves 4

INGREDIENTS

300 g/10^1/$_2$ oz boneless, skinless chicken breasts
1 tbsp cornflour (cornstarch)
1 tsp sesame oil
1 tbsp hoisin sauce
1 tsp light soy sauce
3 garlic cloves, crushed
2 tbsp vegetable oil

75 g/2^3/$_4$ oz/^{3}/$_4$ cup unsalted cashew nuts
25 g/1 oz mangetout (snow peas)
1 celery stick, sliced
1 onion, cut into 8 pieces
60 g/2 oz beansprouts

1 red (bell) pepper, seeded and diced

SAUCE:
2 tsp cornflour (cornstarch)
2 tbsp hoisin sauce
200 ml/7 fl oz/^{7}/$_8$ cup chicken stock

1 Trim any fat from the chicken breasts and cut the meat into thin strips. Place the chicken in a large bowl. Sprinkle with the cornflour (cornstarch) and toss to coat the chicken strips in it, shaking off any excess. Mix together the sesame oil, hoisin sauce, soy sauce and 1 garlic clove. Pour this mixture over the chicken, turning to coat. Marinate for 20 minutes.

2 Heat half of the vegetable oil in a preheated wok. Add the cashew nuts and stir-fry for 1 minute, until browned. Add the mangetout (snow peas), celery, the remaining garlic, the onion, bean-sprouts and red (bell) pepper and cook, stirring occasionally, for 2–3 minutes. Remove the vegetables from the wok with a slotted spoon, set aside and keep warm.

3 Heat the remaining oil in the wok. Remove the chicken from the marinade and stir-fry for 3–4 minutes. Return the vegetables to the wok.

4 To make the sauce, mix the cornflour (cornstarch), hoisin sauce and chicken stock and pour into the wok. Bring to the boil, stirring until thickened and clear. Serve.

Chicken Chop Suey

Serves 4

INGREDIENTS

4 tbsp light soy sauce

2 tsp light brown sugar

500 g/1 1/4 lb skinless, boneless
   chicken breasts

3 tbsp vegetable oil

2 onions, quartered

2 garlic cloves, crushed

350 g/12 oz beansprouts

3 tsp sesame oil

1 tbsp cornflour (cornstarch)

3 tbsp water

425 ml/3/4 pint/2 cups
   chicken stock

shredded leek, to garnish

1 Mix the soy sauce and sugar together, stirring until the sugar has dissolved.

2 Trim any fat from the chicken and cut the meat into thin strips. Place the chicken strips in a shallow glass dish and spoon the soy mixture over them, turning to coat. Leave to marinate in the refrigerator for 20 minutes.

3 Heat the oil in a preheated wok. Add the chicken and stir-fry for 2–3 minutes, until golden brown.

4 Add the onions and garlic and cook for a further 2 minutes. Add the beansprouts, cook for a further 4–5 minutes, then add the sesame oil.

5 Blend the cornflour (cornstarch) with the water to form a smooth paste. Pour the stock into the wok, together with the cornflour (cornstarch) paste and bring to the boil, stirring constantly until the sauce is thickened and clear. Transfer to a warm serving dish, garnish with shredded leek and serve immediately.

VARIATION

This recipe may be made with strips of lean steak, pork or with mixed vegetables. Change the type of stock accordingly.

Chicken with Yellow Bean Sauce

Serves 4

INGREDIENTS

450 g/1 lb skinless, boneless
    chicken breasts
1 egg white, beaten
1 tbsp cornflour (cornstarch)
1 tbsp rice wine vinegar
1 tbsp light soy sauce

1 tsp caster (superfine) sugar
3 tbsp vegetable oil
1 garlic clove, crushed
1-cm/^{1}/2-inch piece fresh root
    ginger, grated

1 green (bell) pepper, seeded
    and diced
2 large mushrooms, sliced
3 tbsp yellow bean sauce
yellow or green (bell) pepper
    strips, to garnish

1 Trim any fat from the chicken. Cut the meat into 2.5-cm/1-inch cubes.

2 Mix the egg white and cornflour (cornstarch) in a shallow bowl. Add the chicken and turn in the mixture to coat. Set aside for 20 minutes.

3 Mix the vinegar, soy sauce and sugar in a bowl.

4 Remove the chicken from the egg white mixture.

5 Heat the oil in a preheated wok, add the chicken and stir-fry for 3–4 minutes, until golden brown. Remove the chicken from the wok with a slotted spoon, set aside and keep warm.

6 Add the garlic, ginger, (bell) pepper and mushrooms to the wok and stir-fry for 1–2 minutes.

7 Add the yellow bean sauce and cook for 1 minute. Stir in the vinegar mixture and return

the chicken to the wok. Cook for 1–2 minutes and serve hot, garnished with (bell) pepper strips.

VARIATION

Black bean sauce would work equally well with this recipe. Although this would affect the appearance of the dish, as it is much darker in colour, the flavours would be compatible.

Crispy Chicken

Serves 4

INGREDIENTS

1.5 kg/3 lb 5 oz oven-ready chicken	2 tsp Chinese five spice powder	850 ml/1 1/2 pints/3 3/4 cups vegetable oil, for frying
2 tbsp clear honey	2 tbsp rice wine vinegar	chilli sauce, to serve

1 Rinse the chicken inside and out under cold running water and pat dry with kitchen paper (paper towels).

2 Bring a large pan of water to the boil and remove from the heat. Place the chicken in the water, cover and set aside for 20 minutes. Remove the chicken from the water and pat dry with kitchen paper (paper towels). Cool and let chill overnight.

3 To make the glaze, mix the honey, Chinese five spice powder and rice wine vinegar.

4 Brush some of the glaze all over the chicken and return to the refrigerator for 20 minutes. Repeat this process until all of the glaze has been used up. Return the chicken to the refrigerator for at least 2 hours after the final coating.

5 Using a cleaver or kitchen knife, open the chicken out by splitting it through the centre through the breast and then cut each half into 4 pieces.

6 Heat the oil for deep-frying in a wok until almost smoking. Reduce the heat and fry each piece of chicken for 5–7 minutes, until golden and cooked through. Remove from the oil with a slotted spoon and drain on absorbent kitchen paper (paper towels).

7 Transfer to a serving dish and serve hot with a little chilli sauce.

COOK'S TIP

If it is easier, use chicken portions instead of a whole chicken. You could also use chicken legs for this recipe, if you prefer.

Spicy Peanut Chicken

Serves 4

INGREDIENTS

300 g/10^1/$_2$ oz skinless,
   boneless chicken breast
2 tbsp peanut oil
125 g/4^1/$_2$ oz/1 cup shelled
   peanuts
1 fresh red chilli, sliced
1 green (bell) pepper, seeded
   and cut into strips

1 tsp sesame oil
fried rice, to serve

SAUCE:
150 ml/^{1}/$_4$ pint/^{2}/$_3$ cup
   chicken stock
1 tbsp Chinese rice wine or
   dry sherry

1 tbsp light soy sauce
1^1/$_2$ tsp light brown sugar
2 garlic cloves, crushed
1 tsp grated fresh root ginger
1 tsp rice wine vinegar

1 Trim any fat from the chicken and cut the meat into 2.5-cm/1-inch cubes. Set aside.

2 Heat the peanut oil in a preheated wok. Add the peanuts and stir-fry for 1 minute. Remove the peanuts with a slotted spoon and set aside.

3 Add the chicken to the wok and cook for 1–2 minutes. Stir in the chilli and (bell) pepper and cook

for 1 minute. Remove from the wok with a slotted spoon.

4 Put half of the peanuts in a food processor and process until almost smooth. Alternatively, place them in a plastic bag and crush with a rolling pin.

5 To make the sauce, add the chicken stock, Chinese rice wine or dry sherry, soy sauce, sugar, garlic, ginger and rice wine vinegar to the wok.

6 Heat the sauce without boiling and stir in the peanut purée, remaining peanuts, chicken, chilli and (bell) pepper. Sprinkle with the sesame oil, stir and cook for 1 minute. Serve hot.

COOK'S TIP

If necessary, process the peanuts with a little of the stock in step 4 to form a softer paste.

Chinese Chicken Salad

Serves 4

INGREDIENTS

225 g/8 oz skinless, boneless
   chicken breasts
2 tsp light soy sauce
1 tsp sesame oil
1 tsp sesame seeds
2 tbsp vegetable oil
125 g/4¹/₂ oz beansprouts

1 red (bell) pepper, seeded and
   thinly sliced
1 carrot, cut into matchsticks
3 baby corn cobs, sliced
snipped chives and carrot
   matchsticks, to garnish

SAUCE:
2 tsp rice wine vinegar
1 tbsp light soy sauce
dash of chilli oil

1 Place the chicken in a shallow glass dish.

2 Mix together the soy sauce and sesame oil and pour over the chicken. Sprinkle with sesame seeds and leave to stand for 20 minutes.

3 Remove the chicken from the marinade and cut the meat into slices.

4 Heat the oil in a preheated wok. Add the chicken and fry for 4-5 minutes, until cooked through and golden brown on both sides. Remove the chicken from the wok with a slotted spoon, set aside and leave to cool.

5 Add the beansprouts, (bell) pepper, carrot and baby corn cobs to the wok and stir-fry for 2–3 minutes. Remove from the wok with a slotted spoon, set aside and leave to cool.

6 To make the sauce, mix the rice wine vinegar, light soy sauce and chilli oil together.

7 Arrange the chicken and vegetables on a serving plate. Spoon the sauce over the salad, garnish and serve.

COOK'S TIP

If you have time, make the sauce and leave to stand for 30 minutes for the flavours to fully develop.

Peking Duck

Serves 4

INGREDIENTS

1.8 kg/4 lb duck
1.75 litres/3 pints/7$^1/_2$ cups
   boiling water
4 tbsp clear honey
2 tsp dark soy sauce

2 tbsp sesame oil
125 ml/4 fl oz/$^1/_2$ cup hoisin
   sauce
125 g/4$^1/_2$ oz/$^2/_3$ cup caster
   (superfine) sugar

125 ml/4 fl oz/$^1/_2$ cup water
carrot strips, to garnish
Chinese pancakes, cucumber
   matchsticks and spring
   onions (scallions), to serve

1 Place the duck on a rack set over a roasting tin (pan) and pour 1.2 litres/2 pints/5 cups of the boiling water over it. Remove the duck and rack and discard the water. Pat dry with paper towels, replace the duck and the rack and set aside for several hours.

2 Mix together the honey, remaining boiling water and soy sauce. Brush the mixture over the skin and inside the duck. Reserve the remaining glaze. Set the duck aside for 1 hour, until the glaze has dried.

3 Coat the duck with another layer of glaze. Let dry and repeat until all of the glaze is used.

4 Heat the oil and add the hoisin sauce, sugar and water. Simmer for 2–3 minutes, until thickened. Cool and refrigerate.

5 Cook the duck in a preheated oven, at 190°C/375°F/Gas Mark 5, for 30 minutes. Turn the duck over and cook for 20 minutes. Turn the duck again and cook for 20–30 minutes, or until cooked through and the skin is crisp.

6 Remove the duck from the oven and set aside for 10 minutes. Meanwhile, heat the pancakes in a steamer for 5–7 minutes. Cut the skin and duck meat into strips, garnish with the carrot strips and serve with the pancakes, sauce, cucumber and spring onions (scallions).

Duck in Spicy Sauce

Serves 4

INGREDIENTS

1 tbsp vegetable oil
1 tsp grated fresh root ginger
1 garlic clove, crushed
1 fresh red chilli, chopped
350 g/12 oz skinless, boneless
   duck meat, cut into strips
125 g/4$^{1}/_{2}$ oz cauliflower, cut
   into florets

60 g/2 oz mangetout (snow
   peas)
60 g/2 oz baby corn cobs,
   halved lengthways
300 ml/$^{1}/_{2}$ pint/1$^{1}/_{4}$ cups
   chicken stock
1 tsp Chinese five spice
   powder

2 tsp Chinese rice wine or dry
   sherry
1 tsp cornflour (cornstarch)
2 tsp water
1 tsp sesame oil

1 Heat the vegetable oil in a preheated wok. Lower the heat slightly and add the ginger, garlic, chilli and duck and stir-fry for 2-3 minutes. Remove with a slotted spoon and set aside.

2 Add the cauliflower florets, mangetout (snow peas) and baby corn cobs to the wok and stir-fry for 2-3 minutes. Pour off any excess oil from the wok and push the vegetables to one side.

3 Return the duck to the wok and pour in the stock. Sprinkle the Chinese five spice powder over the top, stir in the Chinese rice wine or sherry and cook over a low heat for about 15 minutes, or until the duck is tender.

4 Blend the cornflour (cornstarch) with the water to form a paste and stir into the wok, together with the sesame oil. Bring to the boil, stirring until the sauce has thickened and cleared.

5 Transfer the duck and spicy sauce to a warm serving dish and serve immediately.

COOK'S TIP

Omit the chilli for a milder dish, or deseed the chilli before adding it to remove some of the heat.

Honey-glazed Duck

Serves 4

INGREDIENTS

1 tsp dark soy sauce	2 tsp cornflour (cornstarch)	TO GARNISH:
2 tbsp clear honey	2 tsp water	celery leaves
1 tsp garlic vinegar	2 large boneless duck breasts,	cucumber wedges
2 garlic cloves, crushed	about 225g/8 oz each	snipped chives
1 tsp ground star anise		

1 Mix the soy sauce, clear honey, garlic vinegar, garlic and star anise. Blend the cornflour (cornstarch) with the water to form a smooth paste and stir it into the mixture.

2 Place the duck breasts in a shallow ovenproof dish. Brush with the soy marinade, turning to coat them completely. Cover and leave to marinate in the refrigerator for at least 2 hours, or overnight.

3 Remove the duck from the marinade and cook in a preheated oven, at 220°C/425°F/Gas Mark 7, for 20–25 minutes, basting frequently with the glaze.

4 Remove the duck from the oven and transfer to a preheated grill (broiler). Grill (broil) for about 3–4 minutes to caramelize the top.

5 Remove the duck from the grill (broiler) pan and cut into thin slices. Arrange the duck slices in a warm serving dish, garnish with celery leaves, cucumber wedges and snipped chives and serve immediately.

COOK'S TIP

If the duck begins to burn slightly while it is cooking in the oven, cover with foil. Check that the duck breasts are cooked through by inserting the point of a sharp knife into the thickest part of the flesh – the juices should run clear.

Duck With Mangoes

Serves 4

INGREDIENTS

2 medium-size ripe mangoes
300 ml/¹/2 pint/1¹/4 cups
   chicken stock
2 garlic cloves, crushed
1 tsp grated fresh root ginger

3 tbsp vegetable oil
2 large skinless duck breasts,
   about 225 g/8 oz each
1 tsp wine vinegar
1 tsp light soy sauce

1 leek, sliced
freshly chopped parsley, to
   garnish

1 Peel the mangoes and cut the flesh from each side of the stones (pits). Cut the flesh into strips.

2 Put half of the mango pieces and the stock in a food processor and process until smooth. Alternatively, press half of the mangoes through a sieve and mix with the stock.

3 Rub the garlic and ginger over the duck. Heat the oil in a wok and cook the duck breasts, turning, until sealed. Reserve the oil in the wok

and remove the duck. Place the duck on a rack set over a roasting tin (pan) and cook in a preheated oven, at 220°C/425°F/Gas Mark 7, for 20 minutes, until cooked through.

4 Meanwhile, place the mango and stock mixture in a pan and add the vinegar and soy sauce. Bring to the boil and cook over a high heat, stirring, until reduced by half.

5 Heat the oil reserved in the wok and stir-fry the leek and remaining mango

for about 1 minute. Remove from the wok, transfer to a serving dish and keep warm.

6 Slice the cooked duck breasts and arrange the slices on top of the leek and mango mixture. Pour the sauce over the duck slices, garnish and serve.

COOK'S TIP

Do not overcook the mango slices in the wok, or stir too vigorously, otherwise they will break up.

Stir-Fried Duck with Broccoli & (Bell) Peppers

Serves 4

INGREDIENTS

1 egg white	1 yellow (bell) pepper, seeded	2 tsp Chinese rice wine or dry
2 tbsp cornflour (cornstarch)	and diced	sherry
450 g/1 lb skinless, boneless	125 g/4^1/2 oz small broccoli	1 tsp light brown sugar
duck meat	florets	125 ml/4 fl oz/^{1}/2 cup chicken
vegetable oil, for deep-frying	1 garlic clove, crushed	stock
1 red (bell) pepper, seeded and	2 tbsp light soy sauce	2 tsp sesame seeds
diced		

1 Beat the egg white and cornflour (cornstarch) together in a mixing bowl.

2 Cut the duck meat into cubes and stir into the egg white mixture. Let stand for 30 minutes.

3 Heat the oil for deep-frying in a wok until almost smoking. Remove the duck from the egg white mixture, add to the wok and fry in the oil for 4–5 minutes, until crisp. Remove the duck from the oil and drain on kitchen paper (paper towels).

4 Add the (bell) peppers and broccoli to the wok and fry for 2–3 minutes. Remove with a slotted spoon and drain on kitchen paper (paper towels).

5 Pour all but 2 tbsp of the oil from the wok and return to the heat. Add the garlic and stir-fry for 30 seconds. Stir in the soy sauce, Chinese rice wine or sherry, sugar and stock and bring to the boil.

6 Stir in the duck and reserved vegetables and cook for 1–2 minutes.

7 Carefully spoon the duck and vegetables on to a warmed serving dish and sprinkle with the sesame seeds. Serve.

Pork Fry with Vegetables

Serves 4

INGREDIENTS

350 g/12 oz lean pork
  fillet (tenderloin)
2 tbsp vegetable oil
2 garlic cloves, crushed
1-cm/^{1}/2-inch piece fresh root
  ginger, cut into slivers
1 carrot, cut into thin strips

1 red (bell) pepper, seeded and
  diced
1 fennel bulb, sliced
25 g/1 oz water chestnuts,
  halved
75 g/2^3/4 oz beansprouts
2 tbsp Chinese rice wine

300 ml/^{1}/2 pint/1^1/4 cups pork
  or chicken stock
pinch of dark brown sugar
1 tsp cornflour (cornstarch)
2 tsp water

1 Cut the pork into thin slices. Heat the oil in a preheated wok. Add the garlic, ginger and pork and stir-fry for 1–2 minutes, until the meat is sealed.

2 Add the carrot, (bell) pepper, fennel and water chestnuts to the wok and stir-fry for 2–3 minutes.

3 Add the beansprouts and stir-fry for 1 minute. Remove the pork and vegetables from the wok and keep warm.

4 Add the Chinese rice wine, pork or chicken stock and sugar to the wok. Blend the cornflour (cornstarch) to a smooth paste with the water and stir it into the sauce. Bring to the boil, stirring, until thickened and clear.

5 Return the meat and vegetables to the wok and cook for 1–2 minutes, until heated through and coated with the sauce. Transfer to a warm serving dish and serve immediately.

COOK'S TIP

Use dry sherry instead of the Chinese rice wine if you have difficulty obtaining it.

Sweet & Sour Pork

Serves 4

INGREDIENTS

150 ml/^{1}/4 pint/^{2}/3 cup
   vegetable oil, for deep-
   frying
225 g/8 oz pork fillet
   (tenderloin), cut into
   1-cm/^{1}/2-inch cubes
1 onion, sliced
1 green (bell) pepper, seeded
   and sliced
225 g/8 oz pineapple pieces
1 small carrot, cut into thin
   strips

25 g/1 oz canned bamboo
   shoots, drained, rinsed and
   halved
rice or noodles, to serve

BATTER:
125 g/4^1/2 oz/1 cup plain (all-
   purpose) flour
1 tbsp cornflour (cornstarch)
1^1/2 tsp baking powder
1 tbsp vegetable oil

SAUCE:
125 g/4^1/2 oz/^{2}/3 cup light
   brown sugar
2 tbsp cornflour (cornstarch)
125 ml/4 fl oz/^{1}/2 cup white
   wine vinegar
2 garlic cloves, crushed
4 tbsp tomato purée (paste)
6 tbsp pineapple juice

1 To make the batter, sift the flour into a bowl, together with the cornflour (cornstarch) and baking powder. Add the oil and stir in enough water to make a thick batter (about 175 ml/ 6 fl oz/ ^{3}/4 cup). Pour the vegetable oil into a wok and heat until almost smoking. Dip the cubes of pork into the batter, and cook in the hot oil, in batches, until the pork is cooked through. Remove the pork from the wok, set aside and keep warm. Drain all but 1 tbsp of oil from the wok and return it to the heat. Add the onion, (bell) pepper, pineapple pieces, carrot and bamboo shoots and stir-fry for 1–2 minutes. Remove from the wok and set aside.

2 Mix all of the sauce ingredients together and pour into the wok. Bring to the boil, stirring until thickened and clear. Cook for 1 minute, then return the pork and vegetables to the wok. Cook for 1–2 minutes, then transfer to a serving plate and serve.

Pork with Plums

Serves 4

INGREDIENTS

450 g/1 lb pork fillet
(tenderloin)
1 tbsp cornflour (cornstarch)
2 tbsp light soy sauce
2 tbsp Chinese rice wine
4 tsp light brown sugar

pinch of ground cinnamon
5 tsp vegetable oil
2 garlic cloves, crushed
2 spring onions (scallions),
chopped
4 tbsp plum sauce

1 tbsp hoisin sauce
150 ml/^{1}/4 pint/ ^{2}/3 cup water
dash of chilli sauce
fried plum quarters and spring
onions (scallions), to
garnish

1 Cut the pork fillet
(tenderloin) into slices.

2 Mix the cornflour
(cornstarch), soy sauce,
rice wine, sugar and
cinnamon together.

3 Place the pork in a
shallow dish and pour
the cornflour (cornstarch)
mixture over it. Cover and
leave to marinate for at
least 30 minutes.

4 Remove the pork
from the dish,
reserving the marinade.

5 Heat the oil in a
preheated wok. Add
the pork and stir-fry for
3–4 minutes, until lightly
coloured.

6 Stir in the garlic, spring
onions (scallions),
plum sauce, hoisin sauce,
water and chilli sauce.
Bring the sauce to the boil.
Reduce the heat, cover and
simmer for 8–10 minutes,
or until the pork is cooked
through and tender.

7 Stir in the reserved
marinade and cook,

stirring, for 5 minutes.
Transfer to a warm serving
dish and garnish with fried
plum quarters and spring
onions (scallions). Serve
immediately.

VARIATION

*Strips of boneless
duck meat may be used
instead of the pork,
if you prefer.*

Deep-fried Pork Fritters

Serves 4

INGREDIENTS

450 g/1 lb pork fillet
  (tenderloin)
2 tbsp peanut oil
200 g/7 oz/1³/4 cups plain
  (all-purpose) flour
2 tsp baking powder
1 egg, beaten

225 ml/8 fl oz/1 cup milk
pinch of chilli powder
vegetable oil, for deep-frying

SAUCE:
2 tbsp dark soy sauce
3 tbsp clear honey

1 tbsp wine vinegar
1 tbsp chopped chives
1 tbsp tomato purée (paste)
chives, to garnish

1 Cut the pork into
2.5-cm/1-inch cubes.

2 Heat the peanut oil in
a preheated wok. Add
the pork and stir-fry for
2-3 minutes, until sealed.
Remove the pork with a
slotted spoon and set aside
until required.

3 Sift the flour into a
bowl and make a well
in the centre. Gradually
beat in the baking powder,
egg, milk and chilli powder
to make a thick batter.

4 Heat the oil for deep-
frying in a wok until
almost smoking, then
reduce the heat slightly.

5 Toss the pork pieces in
the batter to coat. Add
the pork to the wok and
deep-fry until golden and
cooked through. Remove
with a slotted spoon and
drain on absorbent kitchen
paper (paper towels).

6 To make the sauce, mix
the soy sauce, honey,
wine vinegar, chives and

tomato purée (paste) and
spoon into a small bowl.

7 Transfer the fritters to
serving dishes, garnish
and serve with the sauce.

COOK'S TIP

*Be careful when heating the
oil for deep-frying. It must
be heated so that it is almost
smoking, then the heat must
be reduced immediately.
Place the pork in the
oil carefully.*

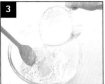

Beef & Broccoli Stir-fry

Serves 4

INGREDIENTS

225 g/8 oz lean steak, trimmed
2 garlic cloves, crushed
dash of chilli oil
1-cm/^{1}/$_{2}$-inch piece fresh root
  ginger, grated

^{1}/$_{2}$ tsp Chinese five spice
  powder
2 tbsp dark soy sauce
2 tbsp vegetable oil
150 g/5 oz broccoli florets
1 tbsp light soy sauce

150 ml/^{1}/$_{4}$ pint/^{2}/$_{3}$ cup beef
  stock
2 tsp cornflour (cornstarch)
4 tsp water
carrot strips, to garnish

1 Cut the steak into thin strips and place in a shallow glass dish. Mix together the garlic, chilli oil, ginger, Chinese five spice powder and soy sauce in a small bowl and pour over the beef, tossing to coat the strips. Leave to marinate in the refrigerator.

2 Heat 1 tbsp of the vegetable oil in a wok. Add the broccoli and stir-fry over a medium heat for 4–5 minutes. Remove from the wok with a slotted spoon and set aside.

3 Heat the remaining oil in the wok. Add the steak together with the marinade, and stir-fry for 2-3 minutes, until the steak is browned and sealed.

4 Return the broccoli to the wok and stir in the soy sauce and stock.

5 Blend the cornflour (cornstarch) with the water to form a smooth paste and stir it into the wok. Bring to the boil, stirring, until thickened and clear. Cook for 1 minute.

6 Transfer the beef and broccoli stir-fry to a warm serving dish, arrange the carrot strips in a lattice on top and serve.

COOK'S TIP

Leave the steak to marinate for several hours for a fuller flavour. Cover and leave to marinate in the refrigerator if preparing in advance.

Marinated Beef With Oyster Sauce

Serves 4

INGREDIENTS

225 g/8 oz lean steak, cut into
  2.5-cm/1-inch cubes
1 tbsp light soy sauce
1 tsp sesame oil
2 tsp Chinese rice wine or
  dry sherry
1 tsp caster (superfine)
  sugar
2 tsp hoisin sauce
1 garlic clove, crushed
$^1/_2$ tsp cornflour (cornstarch)

green (bell) pepper slices,
  to garnish
rice or noodles, to serve

SAUCE:
2 tbsp dark soy sauce
1 tsp caster (superfine) sugar
$^1/_2$ tsp cornflour (cornstarch)
3 tbsp oyster sauce
8 tbsp water
2 tbsp vegetable oil

3 garlic cloves, crushed
1-cm/$^1/_2$-inch piece fresh root
  ginger, grated
8 baby corn cobs, halved
  lengthways
$^1/_2$ green (bell) pepper, seeded
  and thinly sliced
25 g/1 oz bamboo shoots,
  drained and rinsed

1 Place the steak in a shallow dish. Mix together the soy sauce, sesame oil, Chinese rice wine or sherry, sugar, hoisin sauce, garlic and cornflour (cornstarch) and pour over the steak, turning it to coat. Cover and marinate for at least 1 hour.

2 To make the sauce, mix the dark soy sauce with the sugar, cornflour (cornstarch), oyster sauce and water. Heat the oil in a wok. Add the steak and the marinade and stir-fry for 2–3 minutes, until sealed and lightly browned.

3 Add the garlic, ginger, baby corn cobs, (bell) pepper and bamboo shoots. Stir in the oyster sauce mixture and bring to the boil. Reduce the heat and cook for 2–3 minutes. Transfer to a warm serving dish, garnish with green (bell) pepper slices and serve immediately.

COOK'S TIP

For a fuller flavour, marinate the beef in the refrigerator overnight.

Spicy Beef

Serves 4

INGREDIENTS

225 g/8 oz fillet steak
2 garlic cloves, crushed
1 tsp powdered star anise
1 tbsp dark soy sauce
spring onion (scallion) tassels,
   to garnish

SAUCE:
2 tbsp vegetable oil
1 bunch spring onions
   (scallions), halved
   lengthways
1 tbsp dark soy sauce

1 tbsp dry sherry
1/4 tsp chilli sauce
150 ml/1/4 pint/2/3 cup water
2 tsp cornflour (cornstarch)
4 tsp water

1 Cut the steak into thin strips and place in a shallow dish.

2 Mix together the garlic, star anise and dark soy sauce in a bowl and pour over the steak strips, turning them to coat thoroughly. Cover and leave to marinate in the refrigerator for at least 1 hour.

3 To make the sauce, heat the oil in a preheated wok. Reduce the heat, add the halved spring onions

(scallions) and stir-fry for 1-2 minutes. Remove from the wok with a slotted spoon and set aside.

4 Add the beef to the wok, together with the marinade, and stir-fry for 3–4 minutes. Return the halved spring onions (scallions) to the wok and add the soy sauce, sherry, chilli sauce and two thirds of the water.

5 Blend the cornflour (cornstarch) with the remaining water and stir

into the wok. Bring to the boil, stirring until the sauce thickens and clears.

6 Transfer to a warm serving dish, garnish with spring onion (scallion) tassels and serve immediately.

COOK'S TIP

Omit the chilli sauce for a milder dish.

Beef & Beans

Serves 4

INGREDIENTS

450 g/1 lb rump or fillet steak,
  cut into 2.5-cm/1-inch
  pieces

MARINADE:
2 tsp cornflour (cornstarch)
2 tbsp dark soy sauce
2 tsp peanut oil

SAUCE:
2 tbsp vegetable oil
3 garlic cloves, crushed
1 small onion, cut into 8
225 g/8 oz thin green beans,
  halved
25 g/1 oz/^{1}/$_4$ cup unsalted
  cashews
25 g/1 oz canned bamboo
  shoots, drained and rinsed

2 tsp dark soy sauce
2 tsp Chinese rice wine or dry
  sherry
125 ml/4 fl oz/^{1}/$_2$ cup beef
  stock
2 tsp cornflour (cornstarch)
4 tsp water
salt and pepper

1 To make the marinade, mix together the cornflour (cornstarch), soy sauce and peanut oil.

2 Place the steak in a shallow glass bowl. Pour the marinade over the steak, turn to coat, cover and marinate in the refrigerator for 30 minutes.

3 To make the sauce, heat the oil in a preheated wok. Add the garlic, onion, beans, cashews and bamboo shoots and stir-fry for 2–3 minutes.

4 Remove the steak from the marinade, drain, add to the wok and stir-fry for 3–4 minutes.

5 Mix the soy sauce, Chinese rice wine or sherry and beef stock together. Blend the cornflour (cornstarch) with the water and add to the soy sauce mixture, mixing to combine.

6 Stir the mixture into the wok and bring the sauce to the boil, stirring until thickened and clear. Reduce the heat and leave to simmer for 2–3 minutes. Season to taste and serve immediately.

Lamb Meatballs

Serves 4

INGREDIENTS

450 g/1 lb minced (ground) lamb	1 tbsp chopped fresh parsley	1 leek, sliced
3 garlic cloves, crushed	25 g/1 oz/^{1}/$_2$ cup fresh white breadcrumbs	1 tbsp cornflour (cornstarch)
2 spring onions (scallions), finely chopped	1 egg, beaten	2 tbsp water
^{1}/$_2$ tsp chilli powder	3 tbsp vegetable oil	300 ml/^{1}/$_2$ pint/1^1/$_4$ cups lamb stock
1 tsp Chinese curry powder	125 g/4^1/$_2$ oz Chinese cabbage, shredded	1 tbsp dark soy sauce
		shredded leek, to garnish

1 Mix the lamb, garlic, spring onions (scallions), chilli powder, Chinese curry powder, parsley and breadcrumbs together in a bowl. Work the egg into the mixture, bringing it together to form a firm mixture. Roll into 16 even-sized balls.

2 Heat the oil in a wok. Add the cabbage and leek and stir-fry for 1 minute. Remove from the wok with a slotted spoon and set aside.

3 Add the meatballs to the wok and fry in batches, turning gently, for 3–4 minutes, until golden.

4 Mix the cornflour (cornstarch) and water together to form a smooth paste. Pour the lamb stock and soy sauce into the wok and cook for 2–3 minutes. Stir in the cornflour (cornstarch) paste. Bring to the boil and cook, stirring constantly, until the sauce is thickened and clear.

5 Return the cabbage and leek to the wok and cook for 1 minute, until heated through. Arrange the cabbage and leek on a warm serving dish, top with the meatballs, garnish with shredded leek and serve immediately.

VARIATION

Use minced (ground) pork or beef instead of the lamb as an alternative.

Lamb with Mushroom Sauce

Serves 4

INGREDIENTS

350 g/12 oz lean boneless
  lamb, such as fillet or loin
2 tbsp vegetable oil
3 garlic cloves, crushed
1 leek, sliced

1 tsp cornflour (cornstarch)
4 tbsp light soy sauce
3 tbsp Chinese rice wine or
  dry sherry
3 tbsp water

$^1/_2$ tsp chilli sauce
175 g/6 oz large mushrooms,
  sliced
$^1/_2$ tsp sesame oil
fresh red chillies, to garnish

1 Cut the lamb into thin strips.

2 Heat the oil in a preheated wok. Add the lamb strips, garlic and leek and stir-fry for about 2-3 minutes.

3 Mix together the cornflour (cornstarch), soy sauce, Chinese rice wine or dry sherry, water and chilli sauce in a bowl and set aside.

4 Add the mushrooms to the wok and stir-fry for 1 minute.

5 Stir in the sauce and cook for 2–3 minutes, or until the lamb is cooked through and tender. Sprinkle the sesame oil over the top and transfer to a warm serving dish. Garnish with red chillies and serve immediately.

COOK'S TIP

Use rehydrated dried Chinese mushrooms obtainable from specialist shops or Chinese supermarkets for a really authentic flavour.

VARIATION

The lamb can be replaced with lean steak or pork fillet (tenderloin) in this classic recipe from Beijing. You could also use 2–3 spring onions (scallions), 1 shallot or 1 small onion instead of the leek, if you prefer.

Lamb with Garlic Sauce

Serves 4

INGREDIENTS

450 g/1 lb lamb fillet or loin
2 tbsp dark soy sauce
2 tsp sesame oil
2 tbsp Chinese rice wine or dry
  sherry

$^1/_2$ tsp Szechuan pepper
4 tbsp vegetable oil
4 garlic cloves, crushed
60 g/2 oz water chestnuts,
  quartered

1 green (bell) pepper, seeded
  and sliced
1 tbsp wine vinegar
1 tbsp sesame oil
rice or noodles, to serve

1 Cut the lamb into 2.5-cm/1-inch pieces and place in a shallow dish.

2 Mix together 1 tbsp of the soy sauce, the sesame oil, Chinese rice wine or sherry and Szechuan pepper. Pour the mixture over the lamb, turning to coat, and leave to marinate for 30 minutes.

3 Heat the vegetable oil in a preheated wok. Remove the lamb from the marinade and add to the wok with the garlic. Stir-fry for 2–3 minutes.

4 Add the water chestnuts and (bell) pepper to the wok and stir-fry for 1 minute.

5 Add the remaining soy sauce and the wine vinegar, mixing well.

6 Add the sesame oil and cook, stirring, for 1–2 minutes, or until the lamb is cooked through.

7 Transfer the lamb and garlic sauce to a warm serving dish and serve immediately with rice or noodles.

COOK'S TIP

Sesame oil is used as a flavouring, rather than for frying, as it burns readily, hence it is added at the end of cooking.

VARIATION

Chinese chives, also known as garlic chives, would make an appropriate garnish for this dish.

Hot Lamb

Serves 4

INGREDIENTS

450 g/1 lb lean, boneless lamb	1 fennel bulb, sliced	1 fresh green chilli, cut into
2 tbsp hoisin sauce	4 tbsp water	thin strips
1 tbsp dark soy sauce		2 tbsp rice wine vinegar
1 garlic clove, crushed	SAUCE:	2 tsp light brown sugar
2 tsp grated fresh root ginger	1 large fresh red chilli, cut into	2 tbsp peanut oil
2 tbsp vegetable oil	thin strips	1 tsp sesame oil
2 onions, sliced		

1 Cut the lamb into 2.5-cm/1-inch cubes and place in a shallow glass dish.

2 Mix together the hoisin sauce, soy sauce, garlic and ginger in a bowl and pour over the lamb, turning to coat well. Leave to marinate in the refrigerator for 20 minutes.

3 Heat the vegetable oil in a preheated wok. Add the lamb and stir-fry for 1–2 minutes.

4 Add the onions and fennel to the wok and cook for a further 2 minutes, or until they are just beginning to brown.

5 Stir in the water, cover and cook for 2–3 minutes.

6 To make the sauce, place the chillies, rice wine vinegar, sugar, peanut oil and sesame oil in a saucepan and cook over a low heat for 3-4 minutes, stirring to combine.

7 Transfer the lamb and onions to a warm serving dish, pour the sauce on top, toss lightly and serve immediately.

VARIATION

Use beef, pork or duck instead of the lamb and vary the vegetables, using leeks or celery instead of the onion and fennel.

Sesame Lamb Stir-Fry

Serves 4

INGREDIENTS

450 g/1 lb boneless lean lamb
2 tbsp peanut oil
2 leeks, sliced
1 carrot, cut into matchsticks

2 garlic cloves, crushed
3 fl oz/85 ml/^{1}/3 cup lamb or
   vegetable stock
2 tsp light brown sugar

1 tbsp dark soy sauce
4^1/2 tsp sesame seeds

1 Cut the lamb into thin strips. Heat the peanut oil in a preheated wok. Add the lamb and stir-fry for 2–3 minutes. Remove the lamb from the wok with a slotted spoon and set aside.

2 Add the leek, carrot and garlic to the wok and stir-fry in the remaining oil for 1–2 minutes. Remove from the wok with a slotted spoon and set aside. Drain any oil from the wok.

3 Place the stock, sugar and soy sauce in the wok and add the lamb.

Cook, stirring constantly to coat the lamb, for 2–3 minutes. Sprinkle the sesame seeds over the top, turning the lamb to coat.

4 Spoon the leek mixture on to a warm serving dish and top with the lamb. Serve immediately.

COOK'S TIP

Be careful not to burn the sugar in the wok when heating and coating the meat, otherwise the flavour of the dish will be spoiled.

VARIATION

This recipe would be equally delicious made with strips of skinless chicken or turkey breast or with prawns (shrimp). The cooking times remain the same.

Vegetables

Vegetables play a very important role in the Chinese diet and are used extensively in all meals. It is perfectly possible to enjoy a meal from a selection of the following recipes contained in this chapter, without including meat or fish.

The Chinese enjoy their vegetables crisp, so cooking times in this chapter reflect this factor in order to bring out the flavours and textures of the ingredients used, as well as preserving the vitamins and the brightness of the colours. There are main course dishes and a variety of side dishes, all of which bring out the full potential of vegetables.

When selecting vegetables for cooking, the Chinese attach great importance to the freshness of the ingredients used. Always buy crisp, firm vegetables, and cook them as soon as possible. Another point to remember is to wash the vegetables just before cutting, in order to avoid losing vitamins in water, and to cook them as soon as they have been cut so that the vitamin content is not lost through evaporation.

Spicy Aubergines (Eggplants)

Serves 4

INGREDIENTS

450 g/1 lb aubergines
(eggplants), rinsed
2 tsp salt
3 tbsp vegetable oil
2 garlic cloves, crushed

2.5-cm/1-inch piece fresh root
ginger, chopped
1 onion, halved and sliced
1 fresh red chilli, sliced
2 tbsp dark soy sauce
1 tbsp hoisin sauce

$^1/_2$ tsp chilli sauce
1 tbsp dark brown sugar
1 tbsp wine vinegar
1 tsp ground Szechuan pepper
300 ml/$^1/_2$ pint/$1^1/_4$ cups
vegetable stock

1 Cut the aubergines (eggplants) into cubes if you are using the larger variety, or cut the smaller type in half. Place the aubergines (eggplants) in a colander and sprinkle with the salt. Let stand for 30 minutes. Rinse the aubergines (eggplants) under cold running water and pat dry with kitchen paper (paper towels).

2 Heat the oil in a preheated wok and add the garlic, ginger, onion and fresh chilli. Stir-fry for 30 seconds and add the aubergines (eggplants). Continue to cook for 1–2 minutes.

3 Add the soy sauce, hoisin sauce, chilli sauce, sugar, wine vinegar, Szechuan pepper and vegetable stock to the wok, reduce the heat and leave to simmer, uncovered, for 10 minutes, or until the aubergines (eggplants) are cooked. Increase the heat and boil to reduce the sauce until thickened enough to coat the aubergines (eggplants). Serve immediately.

COOK'S TIP

Sprinkling the aubergines (eggplants) with salt and letting them stand removes the bitter juices, which would otherwise taint the flavour of the dish.

Fried Tofu (Bean Curd) & Vegetables

Serves 4

INGREDIENTS

450 g/1 lb tofu (bean curd)
150 ml/¼ pint/⅔ cup
　vegetable oil
1 leek, sliced
4 baby corn cobs, halved
　lengthways
60 g/2 oz mangetout (snow
　peas)

1 red (bell) pepper, seeded and
　diced
60 g/2 oz canned bamboo
　shoots, drained and rinsed
rice or noodles, to serve

SAUCE:
1 tbsp Chinese rice wine or
　dry sherry

4 tbsp oyster sauce
3 tsp light soy sauce
2 tsp caster (superfine) sugar
pinch of salt
50 ml/2 fl oz/¼ cup vegetable
　stock
1 tsp cornflour (cornstarch)
2 tsp water

1 Rinse the tofu (bean curd) in cold water and pat dry with kitchen paper (paper towels). Cut the tofu (bean curd) into 2.5-cm/1-inch cubes.

2 Heat the oil in a preheated wok until almost smoking. Reduce the heat, add the tofu (bean curd) and stir-fry until golden brown. Remove from the wok with a slotted spoon and drain on absorbent kitchen paper (paper towels).

3 Pour all but 2 tbsp of the oil from the wok and return to the heat. Add the leek, corn cobs, mangetout (snow peas), (bell) pepper and bamboo shoots and stir-fry for 2–3 minutes.

4 Add the Chinese rice wine or sherry, oyster sauce, soy sauce, sugar, salt and vegetable stock to the wok and bring to the boil. Blend the cornflour (cornstarch) with the water to form a smooth paste and stir it into the sauce. Bring the sauce to the boil and cook, stirring constantly, until thickened and clear.

5 Stir the tofu (bean curd) into the mixture in the wok and cook for about 1 minute until hot. Serve with rice or noodles.

Tofu (Bean Curd) Casserole

Serves 4

INGREDIENTS

450 g/1 lb tofu (bean curd)	2 garlic cloves, thinly sliced	3 tbsp hoisin sauce
2 tbsp peanut oil	450 g/1 lb baby spinach	1/2 tsp chilli powder
8 spring onions (scallions), cut into batons	rice, to serve	1 tbsp sesame oil
2 celery sticks, sliced	SAUCE:	
125 g/4 1/2 oz broccoli florets	425 ml/3/4 pint/2 cups vegetable stock	
125 g/4 1/2 oz courgettes (zucchini), sliced	2 tbsp light soy sauce	

1 Cut the tofu (bean curd) into 2.5-cm/ 1-inch cubes and set aside.

2 Heat the oil in a preheated wok. Add the spring onions (scallions), celery, broccoli, courgettes (zucchini), garlic, spinach and tofu (bean curd) and stir-fry for 3–4 minutes.

3 To make the sauce, mix together the vegetable stock, soy sauce, hoisin sauce, chilli powder and sesame oil in a flameproof casserole and bring to the boil. Add the vegetables and tofu (bean curd), reduce the heat, cover and simmer for 10 minutes.

4 Transfer to a warm serving dish and serve with rice.

COOK'S TIP

This recipe has a green vegetable theme, but alter the colour and flavour by adding your favourite vegetables, if you prefer.

VARIATION

Add 75 g/3 oz fresh or canned and drained straw mushrooms with the vegetables in step 2.

Marinated Beansprouts & Vegetables

Serves 4

INGREDIENTS

450 g/1 lb beansprouts
2 fresh red chillies, seeded and finely chopped
1 red (bell) pepper, seeded and thinly sliced

1 green (bell) pepper, seeded and thinly sliced
60 g/2 oz water chestnuts, quartered
1 celery stick, sliced

3 tbsp rice wine vinegar
2 tbsp light soy sauce
2 tbsp chopped chives
1 garlic clove, crushed
pinch of Chinese curry powder

1 Place the beansprouts, chilli, (bell) peppers, water chestnuts and celery in a bowl and mix well.

2 Mix together the rice wine vinegar, soy sauce, chives, garlic and Chinese curry powder in a bowl and pour over the prepared vegetables. Toss to mix thoroughly.

3 Cover the salad and leave to chill for at least 3 hours. Drain the vegetables thoroughly, transfer to a serving dish and serve.

COOK'S TIP

There are hundreds of varieties of chillies and it is not always possible to tell how hot they are going to be. As a general rule, dark green chillies are hotter than light green and red chillies. Thin, pointed chillies are usually hotter than fatter, blunter chillies. However, there are always exceptions and even chillies from the same plant can vary considerably in their degree of spiciness.

COOK'S TIP

This dish is delicious with Chinese roasted meats or served with the marinade and noodles.

Honey-fried Chinese Leaves (Cabbage)

Serves 4

INGREDIENTS

450 g/1 lb Chinese leaves
(cabbage)
1 tbsp peanut oil
1-cm/^{1}/2-inch piece fresh root
ginger, grated
2 garlic cloves, crushed

1 fresh red chilli, sliced
1 tbsp Chinese rice wine or dry
sherry
4 ^{1}/2 tsp light soy sauce
1 tbsp clear honey

125 ml/4 fl oz/^{1}/2 cup orange
juice
1 tbsp sesame oil
2 tsp sesame seeds
orange zest, to garnish

1 Separate the Chinese leaves (cabbage) and shred them finely.

2 Heat the peanut oil in a preheated wok. Add the ginger, garlic and chilli to the wok and stir-fry the mixture for 30 seconds.

3 Add the Chinese leaves (cabbage), Chinese rice wine or sherry, soy sauce, honey and orange juice to the wok. Reduce the heat and leave to simmer for 5 minutes.

4 Add the sesame oil, sprinkle the sesame seeds on top and mix to combine. Transfer to a warm serving dish, garnish with the orange zest and serve immediately.

COOK'S TIP

Single-flower honey has a better, more individual flavour than blended honey. Acacia honey is typically Chinese, but you could also try clover, lemon blossom, lime flower or orange blossom.

VARIATION

Use a cabbage, such as Savoy, instead of Chinese leaves (cabbage) if they are unavailable. The flavour will be slightly different and the colour darker, but it will still taste just as delicious.

Green Stir-fry

Serves 4

INGREDIENTS

2 tbsp peanut oil
2 garlic cloves, crushed
1/2 tsp ground star anise
1 tsp salt
350 g/12 oz pak choi,
  shredded

225 g/8 oz baby spinach
25 g/1 oz mangetout (snow
  peas)
1 celery stick, sliced
1 green (bell) pepper, seeded
  and sliced

50 ml/2 fl oz/1/4 cup vegetable
  stock
1 tsp sesame oil

1 Heat the peanut oil in a preheated wok.

2 Add the crushed garlic to the wok and stir-fry for about 30 seconds. Stir in the star anise, salt, pak choi, spinach, mangetout (snow peas), celery and green (bell) pepper and stir-fry for 3–4 minutes.

3 Add the stock, cover and cook for 3–4 minutes.

4 Remove the lid from the wok and stir in the sesame oil. Mix together thoroughly

5 Transfer the stir-fry to a warm serving dish and serve.

COOK'S TIP

Serve this dish as part of a vegetarian meal or alternatively, with roast meats for non-vegetarians.

COOK'S TIP

Star anise is an important ingredient in Chinese cuisine. The attractive star-shaped pods are often used whole to add a decorative garnish to dishes. The flavour is similar to liquorice, but with spicy undertones and is quite strong. Together with cassia, cloves, fennel seeds and Szechuan pepper, dried star anise is used to make Chinese five spice powder.

Crisp Fried Cabbage & Almonds

Serves 4

INGREDIENTS

1.2 kg/2 lb pak choi or spring
    greens (collard greens)
700 ml/1¼ pints/3 cups
    vegetable oil

75 g/2¾ oz/¾ cup blanched
    almonds
1 tsp salt
1 tbsp light brown sugar

pinch of ground cinnamon

1 Separate the leaves
from the pak choi or
spring greens (collard
greens) and rinse them
well. Pat dry with kitchen
paper (paper towels).

2 Shred the greens into
thin strips, using a
sharp knife.

3 Heat the vegetable oil
in a preheated wok
until it is almost smoking.

4 Reduce the heat and
add the greens. Cook
for 2–3 minutes, or until
the greens begin to float in
the oil and are crisp.

5 Remove the greens
from the oil with a
slotted spoon and leave to
drain thoroughly on
absorbent kitchen paper
(paper towels).

6 Add the almonds to the
oil in the wok and cook
for 30 seconds. Remove the
almonds from the oil with a
slotted spoon.

7 Mix the salt, sugar and
cinnamon together and
sprinkle on to the greens.
Toss the almonds into the
greens. Transfer to a warm
serving dish and serve
immediately.

COOK'S TIP

*Ensure that the greens are
completely dry before adding
them to the oil, otherwise it
will spit. The greens will
not become crisp if they are
wet when placed in the oil.*

Creamy Green Vegetables

Serves 4

INGREDIENTS

450 g/1 lb Chinese leaves (cabbage), shredded	300 ml/$^{1}/_{2}$ pint/1$^{1}/_{4}$ cups vegetable stock	2 tbsp single (light) cream or natural (unsweetened) yogurt
2 tbsp peanut oil	1 tbsp light soy sauce	1 tbsp chopped coriander (cilantro)
2 leeks, shredded	2 tsp cornflour (cornstarch)	
4 garlic cloves, crushed	4 tsp water	

1 Blanch the Chinese leaves (cabbage) in boiling water for 30 seconds. Drain, rinse in cold water, then drain thoroughly again.

2 Heat the oil in a preheated wok and add the Chinese leaves (cabbage), leeks and garlic. Stir-fry for 2–3 minutes.

3 Add the vegetable stock and soy sauce to the wok, reduce the heat to low, cover and simmer for 10 minutes, or until the vegetables are tender.

4 Remove the vegetables from the wok with a slotted spoon and set aside. Bring the stock to the boil and boil vigorously until reduced by about half.

5 Blend the cornflour (cornstarch) with the water and stir the mixture into the stock. Bring to the boil, and cook, stirring constantly, until thickened and clear.

6 Reduce the heat and stir in the vegetables and cream or yogurt. Cook over a low heat for 1 minute.

7 Transfer to a serving dish, sprinkle over the chopped coriander (cilantro) and serve.

COOK'S TIP

Do not boil the sauce once the cream or yogurt has been added, as it will separate.

Stir-Fried Cucumber with Chillies

Serves 4

INGREDIENTS

2 medium cucumbers
2 tsp salt
1 tbsp vegetable oil
2 garlic cloves, crushed

1-cm/1/2-inch fresh root
    ginger, grated
2 fresh red chillies, chopped
2 spring onions (scallions),
    chopped

1 tsp yellow bean sauce
1 tbsp clear honey
125 ml/4 fl oz/1/2 cup water
1 tsp sesame oil

1 Peel the cucumbers and cut in half lengthways. Scrape the seeds from the centre with a teaspoon and discard.

2 Cut the cucumber into strips and place on a plate. Sprinkle the salt over the cucumber strips and set aside for 20 minutes. Rinse well under cold running water and pat dry with absorbent kitchen paper (paper towels).

3 Heat the oil in a preheated wok until it is almost smoking. Lower the heat slightly and add the garlic, ginger, chilli and spring onions (scallions) and stir-fry for 30 seconds.

4 Add the cucumbers to the wok, together with the yellow bean sauce and honey. Stir-fry for a further 30 seconds.

5 Add the water and cook over a high heat until most of the water has evaporated.

6 Sprinkle the sesame oil over the cucumber and chilli stir-fry. Transfer to a warm serving dish and serve immediately.

COOK'S TIP

The cucumber is sprinkled with salt and left to stand in order to draw out the excess water, thus preventing a soggy meal!

Spicy Mushrooms

Serves 4

INGREDIENTS

2 tbsp peanut oil
2 garlic cloves, crushed
3 spring onions (scallions), chopped
300 g/10 oz button mushrooms

2 large open-cap mushrooms, sliced
125 g/4½ oz oyster mushrooms
1 tsp chilli sauce
1 tbsp dark soy sauce
1 tbsp hoisin sauce

1 tbsp wine vinegar
½ tsp ground Szechuan pepper
1 tbsp dark brown sugar
1 tsp sesame oil
chopped parsley, to garnish

1 Heat the oil in a wok until almost smoking. Reduce the heat slightly, add the garlic and spring onions (scallions) and stir-fry for 30 seconds.

2 Add the mushrooms, chilli sauce, soy sauce, hoisin sauce, vinegar, pepper and sugar and stir-fry for 4–5 minutes, or until the mushrooms are cooked through.

3 Sprinkle the sesame oil on top. Transfer to a warm serving dish, garnish with parsley and serve immediately.

COOK'S TIP

This dish is ideal served with rich meat or fish dishes.

COOK'S TIP

Chinese mushrooms are used more for their unusual texture than for their flavour. Wood (tree) ears are widely used and are available dried from Chinese food stores. They should be rinsed, soaked in warm water for about 20 minutes and rinsed again before use. Straw mushrooms are available fresh or canned from Chinese food stores and some supermarkets. They have a slippery texture.

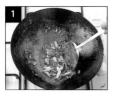

Garlic Spinach

Serves 4

INGREDIENTS

900 g/2 lb fresh spinach
2 tbsp peanut oil
2 garlic cloves, crushed

1 tsp chopped lemon grass
pinch of salt
1 tbsp dark soy sauce

2 tsp brown sugar

1 Carefully remove the stems from the spinach. Rinse the spinach leaves and drain them thoroughly, patting them dry with absorbent kitchen paper (paper towels).

2 Heat the oil in a preheated wok until it is almost smoking.

3 Reduce the heat slightly, add the garlic and lemon grass and stir-fry for 30 seconds.

4 Add the spinach and salt to the wok and stir-fry for 2–3 minutes, or until the spinach has wilted.

5 Stir in the dark soy sauce and brown sugar and cook for a further 3–4 minutes. Transfer to a warm serving dish and serve immediately.

COOK'S TIP

Lemon grass is widely used in Asian cooking. It is available fresh, dried and canned or bottled. Dried lemon grass must be soaked for 2 hours before using. The stems are hard and are usually used whole and removed from the dish before serving. The roots can be crushed or finely chopped.

COOK'S TIP

Use baby spinach, if possible, as the leaves have a better flavour and look more appealing. If using baby spinach, the stems may be left intact.

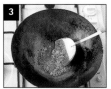

Chinese Fried Vegetables

Serves 4

INGREDIENTS

2 tbsp peanut oil
350 g/12 oz broccoli florets
1 tbsp chopped fresh root
    ginger
2 onions, cut into 8
3 celery sticks, sliced
175 g/6 oz baby spinach

125 g/4^1/2 oz mangetout
    (snow peas)
6 spring onions (scallions),
    quartered
2 garlic cloves, crushed
2 tbsp light soy sauce
2 tsp caster (superfine) sugar

2 tbsp dry sherry
1 tbsp hoisin sauce
150 ml/^{1}/4 pint/^{2}/3 cup
    vegetable stock

1 Heat the peanut oil in a preheated wok until it is almost smoking.

2 Add the broccoli florets, ginger, onions and celery and stir-fry for 1 minute.

3 Add the spinach, mangetout (snow peas), spring onions (scallions) and garlic and stir-fry for 3–4 minutes.

4 Mix the soy sauce, sugar, sherry, hoisin sauce and stock and pour into the wok, mixing well to coat the vegetables. Cover and cook over a medium heat for 2–3 minutes, or until the vegetables are cooked through, but still crisp. Transfer to a serving dish and serve.

VARIATION

Any vegetables may be used in this recipe, depending on your preference and their seasonal availability.

COOK'S TIP

You could use this mixture to fill Chinese pancakes. They are available from Chinese food stores and can be reheated in a steamer in 2–3 minutes.

Vegetable Chop Suey

Serves 4

INGREDIENTS
---

1 yellow (bell) pepper, seeded	60 g/2 oz mangetout (snow	2 tbsp light soy sauce
1 red (bell) pepper, seeded	peas)	125 ml/4 fl oz/^{1}/2 cup
1 carrot	2 tbsp peanut oil	vegetable stock
1 courgette (zucchini)	3 garlic cloves, crushed	
1 fennel bulb	1 tsp grated fresh root ginger	
1 onion	125 g/4^1/2 oz beansprouts	
	2 tsp light brown sugar	

1 Cut the (bell) peppers, carrot, courgette (zucchini) and fennel into thin slices. Cut the onion into quarters and then cut each quarter in half. Slice the mangetout (snow peas) diagonally to create the maximum surface area.

2 Heat the oil in a preheated wok until it is almost smoking. Add the garlic and ginger and stir-fry for 30 seconds. Add the onion and stir-fry for a further 30 seconds.

3 Add the (bell) peppers, carrot, courgette (zucchini), fennel and mangetout (snow peas) and stir-fry for 2 minutes.

4 Add the beansprouts to the wok and stir in the sugar, soy sauce and stock. Reduce the heat and simmer for 1–2 minutes, until the vegetables are tender and coated in the sauce.

5 Transfer the vegetables and sauce to a serving dish and serve immediately.

COOK'S TIP

Use any combination of colourful vegetables that you have to hand to make this versatile dish.

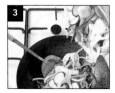

Vegetable Sesame Stir-fry

Serves 4

INGREDIENTS

2 tbsp vegetable oil
3 garlic cloves, crushed
1 tbsp sesame seeds, plus
    extra to garnish
2 celery sticks, sliced
2 baby corn cobs, sliced
60 g/2 oz button mushrooms

1 leek, sliced
1 courgette (zucchini), sliced
1 small red (bell) pepper, sliced
1 fresh green chilli, sliced
60 g/2 oz Chinese leaves
    (cabbage), shredded
1/2 tsp Chinese curry powder

2 tbsp light soy sauce
1 tbsp Chinese rice wine or dry
    sherry
1 tsp sesame oil
1 tsp cornflour (cornstarch)
4 tbsp water

1 Heat the oil in a preheated wok until it is almost smoking. Lower the heat slightly, add the garlic and sesame seeds and stir-fry for 30 seconds.

2 Add the celery, baby corn, mushrooms, leek, courgette (zucchini), (bell) pepper, chilli and Chinese leaves (cabbage) and stir-fry for 4–5 minutes, or until softened.

3 Mix the Chinese curry powder, soy sauce, Chinese rice wine or sherry, sesame oil, cornflour (cornstarch) and water and stir the mixture into the wok. Bring to the boil and cook, stirring, until the sauce thickens and clears. Cook for 1 minute, spoon into a warm serving dish, sprinkle sesame seeds on top and serve.

VARIATION

You could substitute oyster sauce for the soy sauce, if you prefer.

COOK'S TIP

The ingredients are fried in vegetable oil in this recipe and not peanut oil as this would overpower the wonderful flavour of the sesame seeds.

Green Bean Stir-fry

Serves 4

INGREDIENTS

450 g/1 lb thin green beans
2 fresh red chillies
2 tbsp peanut oil
$^{1}/_{2}$ tsp ground star anise

1 garlic clove, crushed
2 tbsp light soy sauce
2 tsp clear honey

$^{1}/_{2}$ tsp sesame oil

1 Cut the green beans in half.

2 Slice the fresh chillies, seeding them first if you prefer a milder dish.

3 Heat the oil in a preheated wok until almost smoking.

4 Lower the heat slightly, add the green beans and stir-fry for 1 minute.

5 Add the sliced red chillies, star anise and garlic to the wok and stir-fry for a further 30 seconds.

6 Mix together the soy sauce, honey and sesame oil and stir into the wok. Cook for 2 minutes, tossing the beans in the sauce to coat. Transfer the beans to a warm serving dish and serve immediately.

COOK'S TIP

This dish makes a great accompaniment to fish or lightly cooked meats with a mild flavour.

VARIATION

This recipe is surprisingly delicious made with Brussels sprouts instead of green beans. Trim the sprouts, then shred them finely. Stir-fry the sprouts in hot oil for 2 minutes, then proceed with the recipe from step 5.

Vegetable Rolls

Serves 4

INGREDIENTS

8 large Chinese leaves
(Chinese cabbage leaves)

FILLING:
2 baby corn cobs, sliced
1 carrot, finely chopped
1 celery stick, chopped

4 spring onions (scallions),
chopped
4 water chestnuts, chopped
2 tbsp unsalted cashews,
chopped
1 garlic clove, chopped
1 tsp grated fresh root ginger

25 g/1 oz canned bamboo
shoots, drained, rinsed and
chopped
1 tsp sesame oil
2 tsp soy sauce

1 Place the Chinese leaves (cabbage leaves) in a large bowl and pour boiling water over them to soften them. Leave for 1 minute and drain thoroughly.

2 Mix together the baby corn cobs, carrot, celery, spring onions (scallions), water chestnuts, cashews, garlic, ginger and bamboo shoots in a bowl.

3 Mix together the sesame oil and soy sauce and add to the vegetables, mixing well.

4 Spread out the Chinese leaves (cabbage leaves) on a board and spoon an equal quantity of the filling mixture on to each leaf.

5 Roll the leaves up, folding in the sides, to make neat parcels. Secure the parcels with cocktail sticks (toothpicks).

6 Place the filled rolls in a small heatproof dish in a steamer, cover and cook for 15–20 minutes, until the parcels are cooked. Serve with a sauce of your choice.

COOK'S TIP

Make the parcels in advance, cover and store in the refrigerator until required, then steam according to the recipe.

Eight Jewel Vegetables

Serves 4

INGREDIENTS

2 tbsp peanut oil
6 spring onions (scallions), sliced
3 garlic cloves, crushed
1 green (bell) pepper, seeded and diced
1 red (bell) pepper, seeded and diced

1 fresh red chilli, sliced
2 tbsp chopped water chestnuts
1 courgette (zucchini), chopped
125 g/4^1/2 oz oyster mushrooms
3 tbsp black bean sauce

2 tsp Chinese rice wine or dry sherry
4 tbsp dark soy sauce
1 tsp dark brown sugar
2 tbsp water
1 tsp sesame oil

1 Heat the peanut oil in a preheated wok until it is almost smoking.

2 Lower the heat slightly, add the spring onions (scallions) and garlic and stir-fry for 30 seconds.

3 Add the (bell) peppers, chilli, water chestnuts and courgette (zucchini) to the wok and stir-fry for 2–3 minutes, or until the vegetables are just beginning to soften.

4 Add the mushrooms, black bean sauce, rice wine or sherry, soy sauce, sugar and water to the wok and stir-fry for 4 minutes.

5 Sprinkle with sesame oil and serve.

VARIATION

Add 225 g/8 oz diced, marinated tofu (bean curd) to this recipe for a main meal for 4 people.

COOK'S TIP

Eight jewels or treasures form a traditional part of the Chinese New Year celebrations, which start in the last week of the old year. The Kitchen God, an important figure, is sent to give a report to heaven, returning on New Year's Eve in time for the feasting.

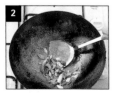

Spicy Vegetarian Fried Triangles

Serves 4

INGREDIENTS

1 tbsp sea salt	2 garlic cloves, crushed	vegetable oil, for deep-frying
4¹/₂ tsp Chinese five spice powder	1 tsp grated fresh root ginger	2 leeks, halved and shredded
3 tbsp light brown sugar	2 x 225 g/8 oz cakes tofu (bean curd)	shredded leek, to garnish

1 Mix the salt, Chinese five spice, sugar, garlic and ginger in a bowl and transfer to a plate.

2 Cut the tofu (bean curd) cakes in half diagonally to form two triangles. Cut each triangle in half and then in half again to form 16 triangles.

3 Roll the tofu (bean curd) triangles in the spice mixture, turning to coat thoroughly. Set aside for 1 hour.

4 Heat the oil for deep-frying in a wok until it

is almost smoking. Reduce the heat slightly, add the tofu (bean curd) triangles and fry for 5 minutes, until golden brown. Remove from the wok with a slotted spoon and set aside.

5 Add the leeks to the wok and stir-fry for 1 minute. Remove from the wok with a slotted spoon and drain on absorbent kitchen paper (paper towels).

6 Arrange the leeks on a warm serving plate and place the fried tofu (bean curd) on top. Garnish with

the fresh shredded leek and serve immediately.

COOK'S TIP

Fry the tofu (bean curd) in batches and keep each batch warm until all of the tofu (bean curd) has been fried and is ready to serve.

Chinese Vegetable Casserole

Serves 4

INGREDIENTS

4 tbsp vegetable oil
2 medium carrots, sliced
1 courgette (zucchini), sliced
4 baby corn cobs, halved
lengthways
125 g/4^{1}/$_{2}$ oz cauliflower
florets
1 leek, sliced

125 g/4^{1}/$_{2}$ oz water chestnuts,
halved
225 g/8 oz tofu (bean curd),
diced
300 ml/^{1}/$_{2}$ pint/1^{1}/$_{4}$ cups
vegetable stock
1 tsp salt
2 tsp dark brown sugar

2 tsp dark soy sauce
2 tbsp dry sherry
1 tbsp cornflour (cornstarch)
2 tbsp water
1 tbsp chopped coriander
(cilantro), to garnish

1 Heat the vegetable oil in a preheated wok until it is almost smoking.

2 Lower the heat slightly, add the carrots, courgette (zucchini), corn cobs, cauliflower florets and leek to the wok and stir-fry for 2–3 minutes.

3 Stir in the water chestnuts, tofu (bean curd), stock, salt, sugar, soy sauce and sherry and bring to the boil. Reduce the heat, cover and simmer for 20 minutes.

4 Blend the cornflour (cornstarch) with the water to form a paste.

5 Remove the lid from the wok and stir in the cornflour (cornstarch) mixture. Bring the sauce to the boil and cook, stirring until it thickens and clears.

6 Transfer the casserole to a warm serving dish, sprinkle with chopped coriander (cilantro) and serve immediately.

COOK'S TIP

If there is too much liquid remaining, boil vigorously for 1 minute before adding the cornflour (cornstarch) to reduce it slightly.

Bamboo Shoots, Ginger & (Bell) Peppers

Serves 4

INGREDIENTS

2 tbsp peanut oil	1 small green (bell) pepper,	1 tbsp light soy sauce
225 g/8 oz canned bamboo	seeded and thinly sliced	2 tsp light brown sugar
shoots, drained and rinsed	1 small yellow (bell) pepper,	2 tsp Chinese rice wine or
2.5-cm/1-inch piece fresh root	seeded and thinly sliced	dry sherry
ginger, finely chopped	1 leek, sliced	1 tsp cornflour (cornstarch)
1 small red (bell) pepper,	125 ml/4 fl oz/$\frac{1}{2}$ cup	2 tsp water
seeded and thinly sliced	vegetable stock	1 tsp sesame oil

1 Heat the peanut oil in a preheated wok.

2 Add the bamboo shoots, ginger, (bell) peppers and leek to the wok and stir-fry for 2–3 minutes.

3 Stir in the stock, soy sauce, sugar and Chinese rice wine or sherry and bring to the boil, stirring. Reduce the heat and simmer for 4–5 minutes, or until the vegetables begin to soften.

4 Blend the cornflour (cornstarch) with the water to form a paste.

5 Stir the cornflour (cornstarch) paste into the wok. Bring to the boil and cook, stirring, until the sauce thickens and clears.

6 Sprinkle the sesame oil over the vegetables and cook for 1 minute. Transfer to a warm serving dish and serve.

COOK'S TIP

Add a chopped fresh red chilli or a few drops of chilli sauce for a spicier dish.

Bamboo Shoots with Spinach

Serves 4

INGREDIENTS

3 tbsp peanut oil
225 g/8 oz spinach, chopped
175 g/6 oz canned bamboo
shoots, drained and rinsed
1 garlic clove, crushed

2 fresh red chillies, sliced
pinch of ground cinnamon
300 ml/$\frac{1}{2}$ pint/1$\frac{1}{4}$ cups
vegetable stock
pinch of sugar

pinch of salt
1 tbsp light soy sauce

1 Heat the peanut oil in a preheated wok.

2 Add the spinach and bamboo shoots to the wok and stir-fry for 1 minute.

3 Add the garlic, chilli and cinnamon to the mixture in the wok and stir-fry for a further 30 seconds.

4 Stir in the vegetable stock, sugar, salt and soy sauce, cover and cook over a medium heat for 5 minutes, or until the

vegetables are cooked through and the sauce has reduced. Transfer the bamboo shoots and spinach to a warm serving dish and serve.

COOK'S TIP

If there is too much liquid after 5 minutes cooking in step 4, blend a little cornflour (cornstarch) with double the quantity of cold water and stir into the sauce.

COOK'S TIP

Fresh bamboo shoots are rarely available in the West and, in any case, are extremely time-consuming to prepare. Canned bamboo shoots are quite satisfactory, as they are used to provide a crunchy texture, rather than for their flavour, which is fairly insipid.

Sweet & Sour Tofu (Bean Curd) with Vegetables

Serves 4

INGREDIENTS

2 celery sticks	2 garlic cloves, crushed	SAUCE:
1 carrot	8 baby corn cobs	2 tbsp light brown sugar
1 green (bell) pepper, seeded	125 g/4^1/2 oz beansprouts	2 tbsp wine vinegar
75 g/3 oz mangetout (snow peas)	450 g/1 lb tofu (bean curd), cubed	225 ml/8 fl oz/1 cup vegetable stock
2 tbsp vegetable oil	rice or noodles, to serve	1 tsp tomato purée (paste)
		1 tbsp cornflour (cornstarch)

1 Thinly slice the celery, cut the carrot into thin strips, dice the (bell) pepper and cut the mangetout (snow peas) in half diagonally.

2 Heat the oil in a preheated wok until it is almost smoking. Reduce the heat slightly, add the garlic, celery, carrot, (bell) pepper, mangetout (snow peas) and corn cobs and stir-fry for 3–4 minutes.

3 Add the beansprouts and tofu (bean curd) to the wok and cook for 2 minutes, stirring well.

4 To make the sauce, combine the sugar, wine vinegar, vegetable stock, tomato purée (paste) and cornflour (cornstarch), stirring well to mix. Stir into the wok, bring to the boil and cook, stirring, until the sauce thickens and clears. Continue to cook for 1 minute. Serve with rice or noodles.

COOK'S TIP

Be careful not to break up the tofu (bean curd) when stirring.

Gingered Broccoli

Serves 4

INGREDIENTS

2 tbsp peanut oil
1 garlic clove, crushed
5-cm/2-inch piece fresh root
    ginger, finely chopped
675 g/1 1/2 lb broccoli florets

1 leek, sliced
75 g/2 3/4 oz water chestnuts,
    halved
1/2 tsp caster (superfine) sugar

125 ml/4 fl oz/1/2 cup
    vegetable stock
1 tsp dark soy sauce
1 tsp cornflour (cornstarch)
2 tsp water

1 Heat the oil in a preheated wok. Add the garlic and ginger and stir-fry for 30 seconds. Add the broccoli, leek and water chestnuts and stir-fry for a further 3–4 minutes.

2 Add the sugar, stock and soy sauce, reduce the heat and simmer for 4–5 minutes, or until the broccoli is almost cooked.

3 Blend the cornflour (cornstarch) with the water to form a smooth paste and stir it into the wok. Bring to the boil and cook, stirring constantly, for 1 minute. Transfer to a serving dish and serve immediately.

COOK'S TIP

If you prefer a slightly milder ginger flavour, cut the ginger into larger strips, stir-fry as described and then remove from the wok and discard.

VARIATION

You could substitute spinach for the broccoli, if you prefer. Trim the woody ends and cut the remainder into 5-cm/2-inch lengths, keeping the stalks and leaves separate. Add the stalks with the leek in step 1 and add the leafy parts 2 minutes later. Reduce the cooking time in step 2 to 3–4 minutes.

Chinese Potato Sticks

Serves 4

INGREDIENTS

650 g/1¹/₂ lb medium-size
   potatoes
8 tbsp vegetable oil
1 fresh red chilli, halved

1 small onion, quartered
2 garlic cloves, halved
2 tbsp soy sauce
pinch of salt

1 tsp wine vinegar
1 tbsp coarse sea salt
pinch of chilli powder

1 Peel the potatoes and cut into thin slices along their length. Cut the slices into matchsticks.

2 Blanch the potato sticks in boiling water for 2 minutes, drain, rinse under cold water and drain well again. Pat thoroughly dry with absorbent kitchen paper (paper towels).

3 Heat the oil in a preheated wok until it is almost smoking. Add the chilli, onion and garlic and stir-fry for 30 seconds. Remove and discard the chilli, onion and garlic.

4 Add the potato sticks to the oil and fry for 3–4 minutes, or until golden.

5 Add the soy sauce, salt and vinegar to the wok, reduce the heat and fry for 1 minute, or until the potatoes are crisp.

6 Remove the potatoes with a slotted spoon and leave to drain on absorbent kitchen paper (paper towels).

7 Transfer the potato sticks to a serving dish, sprinkle with the sea salt and chilli powder and serve.

VARIATION

Sprinkle other flavourings over the cooked potato sticks, such as curry powder, or serve with a chilli dip.

Cucumber & Beansprout Salad

Serves 4

INGREDIENTS

350 g/12 oz beansprouts
1 small cucumber
1 green (bell) pepper, seeded
    and cut into matchsticks
1 carrot, cut into matchsticks

2 tomatoes, finely chopped
1 celery stick, cut into
    matchsticks
1 garlic clove, crushed
dash of chilli sauce

2 tbsp light soy sauce
1 tsp wine vinegar
2 tsp sesame oil
16 fresh chives

1 Blanch the beansprouts in boiling water for 1 minute. Drain well and rinse under cold water. Drain thoroughly again.

2 Cut the cucumber in half lengthways. Scoop out the seeds with a teaspoon and discard. Cut the flesh into matchsticks and mix with the beansprouts, green (bell) pepper, carrot, tomatoes and celery.

3 Mix together the garlic, chilli sauce, soy sauce, vinegar and sesame oil. Pour the dressing over the vegetables, tossing well to coat. Spoon on to 4 individual serving plates. Garnish with fresh chives and serve.

COOK'S TIP

The vegetables may be prepared in advance, but do not assemble the dish until just before serving, otherwise the beansprouts will discolour.

VARIATION

You could substitute 350 g/12 oz cooked, cooled green beans or mangetout (snow peas) for the cucumber. Vary the beansprouts for a different flavour. Try aduki (adzuki) bean or alfalfa sprouts, as well as the better-known mung and soya beansprouts.

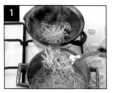  

Rice & Noodles

No Chinese cookbook would be complete without recipes for rice and noodle dishes. Many people believe that they should always serve rice with a savoury meal, and although it is often an excellent choice, there are many wonderful noodle dishes that can be served in its place.

Nevertheless, this chapter includes some delicious rice recipes which may be served as accompaniments or on their own. The Chinese use long-grain, short-grain or glutinous rice, and real experts would never use 'easy-cook' rice. Use whichever you are able to obtain for the recipes that follow and enjoy them! Fried rice is the most popular rice in Western restaurants, and so several variations have been included in this chapter.

A wide variety of noodles are available, made from wheat, buckwheat or rice flours. Noodles are used to their full potential in this chapter to bring you delicious accompaniments and main meal dishes.

Egg Fried Rice

Serves 4

INGREDIENTS

150 g/5¹/2 oz/²/3 cup long-
 grain rice
3 eggs, beaten
2 tbsp vegetable oil
2 garlic cloves, crushed

4 spring onions (scallions),
 chopped
125 g/4¹/2 oz/1 cup cooked
 peas
1 tbsp light soy sauce

pinch of salt
shredded spring onion
 (scallion), to garnish

1 Cook the rice in a
 saucepan of boiling
water for 10-12 minutes,
until almost cooked, but
not soft. Drain well, rinse
under cold water and drain
thoroughly again.

2 Place the beaten eggs
 in a saucepan and cook
over a gentle heat, stirring
until softly scrambled.

3 Heat the oil in a
 preheated wok. Add
the garlic, spring onions
(scallions) and peas and
sauté, stirring occasionally,
for 1-2 minutes.

4 Stir the rice into the
 mixture in the pan,
mixing to combine.

5 Add the eggs, soy sauce
 and salt to the wok and
stir to mix the egg in well.

6 Transfer to serving
 dishes and garnish with
the spring onion (scallion).

COOK'S TIP

*The rice is rinsed
under cold water to wash
out the starch and prevent it
from sticking together.*

VARIATION

*You may choose to add
prawns (shrimp), ham or
chicken in step 3,
if you wish.*

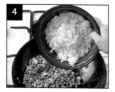

Fried Rice with Pork

Serves 4

INGREDIENTS

150 g/5¹/₂ oz/²/₃ cup long-
   grain rice
3 tbsp peanut oil
1 large onion, cut into 8
225 g/8 oz pork tenderloin,
   thinly sliced

2 open-cap mushrooms, sliced
2 garlic cloves, crushed
1 tbsp light soy sauce
1 tsp light brown sugar
2 tomatoes, skinned, seeded
   and chopped

60 g/2 oz/¹/₂ cup cooked peas
2 eggs, beaten

1 Cook the rice in a saucepan of boiling water for 15 minutes, until tender, but not soft. Drain well, rinse under cold running water and drain again thoroughly.

2 Heat the oil in a preheated wok. Add the sliced onion and pork and stir-fry for 3-4 minutes, or until just beginning to colour.

3 Add the mushrooms and garlic to the wok and stir-fry for 1 minute.

4 Add the soy sauce and sugar to the mixture in the wok and stir-fry for a further 2 minutes.

5 Stir in the rice, tomatoes and peas, mixing well. Transfer the mixture to a warmed dish.

6 Stir the eggs into the wok and cook, stirring for 2-3 minutes, until just beginning to set.

7 Return the rice mixture to the wok and mix well. Transfer to serving dishes and serve immediately.

COOK'S TIP

You can cook the rice in advance and chill or freeze it until required.

Vegetable Fried Rice

Serves 4

INGREDIENTS

125 g/5 oz/²/₃ cup long-grain
  white rice
3 tbsp peanut oil
2 garlic cloves, crushed
¹/₂ tsp Chinese five spice
  powder

60 g/2 oz/¹/₃ cup green beans
1 green (bell) pepper, seeded
  and chopped
4 baby corn cobs, sliced
25 g/1 oz bamboo shoots,
  chopped

3 tomatoes, skinned, seeded
  and chopped
60 g/2 oz/¹/₂ cup cooked peas
1 tsp sesame oil

1 Cook the rice in a
saucepan of boiling
water for 15 minutes.
Drain well, rinse under
cold running water and
drain thoroughly again.

2 Heat the peanut oil in
a preheated wok.

3 Add the garlic and
Chinese five spice and
stir-fry for 30 seconds.

4 Add the green beans,
(bell) pepper and
corn cobs and stir-fry
for 2 minutes.

5 Stir the bamboo
shoots, tomatoes, peas
and rice into the mixture in
the wok and stir-fry for
1 minute.

6 Sprinkle the vegetable
fried rice with sesame
oil and transfer to serving
dishes. Serve immediately.

VARIATION

*You could add cashew nuts,
dry-fried until lightly
browned, in step 5
if you prefer.*

COOK'S TIP

*Use a selection
of vegetables of your choice
in this recipe, cutting them
to a similar size in order
to ensure that they
cook in the same
amount of time.*

Green-fried Rice

Serves 4

INGREDIENTS

150 g/5¹/2 oz/²/3 cup long-
   grain rice
2 tbsp vegetable oil
2 garlic cloves, crushed

1 tsp grated fresh root ginger
1 carrot, cut into matchsticks
1 courgette (zucchini), diced
225 g/8 oz baby spinach

2 tsp light soy sauce
2 tsp light brown sugar

1 Cook the rice in a saucepan of boiling water for 15 minutes. Drain the rice well, rinse under cold running water and then rinse the rice thoroughly again.

2 Heat the vegetable oil in a preheated wok.

3 Add the garlic and ginger to the wok and stir-fry for about 30 seconds.

4 Add the carrot and courgette (zucchini) to the mixture in the wok and stir-fry for 2 minutes.

5 Add the baby spinach and stir-fry for 1 minute, until wilted.

6 Add the rice, soy sauce and sugar to the wok and mix together well.

7 Transfer the green-fried rice to warm serving dishes and serve immediately.

COOK'S TIP

Light soy sauce has more flavour than the sweeter, dark soy sauce, which gives the food a rich, reddish colour.

VARIATION

Chinese leaves may be used instead of the spinach, giving a lighter green colour to the dish.

Special Fried Rice

Serves 4

INGREDIENTS

150 g/5¹/2 oz/²/3 cup long-
grain rice
2 tbsp vegetable oil
2 eggs, beaten
2 garlic cloves, crushed

1 tsp grated fresh root ginger
3 spring onions (scallions),
sliced
75 g/3 oz/³/4 cup cooked peas
150 g/5¹/2 oz/²/3 cup
beansprouts

225 g/8 oz/1¹/3 cups shredded
ham
150 g/5¹/2 oz peeled, cooked
prawns (shrimp)
2 tbsp light soy sauce

1 Cook the rice in a saucepan of boiling water for 15 minutes. Drain well, rinse under cold water and drain thoroughly again.

2 Heat 1 tablespoon of the oil in a preheated wok and add the beaten eggs and a further 1 teaspoon of oil. Tilt the wok so that the egg covers the base to make a thin pancake. Cook until lightly browned on the underside, then flip the pancake over and cook on the other side for 1 minute. Remove from the wok and leave to cool.

3 Heat the remaining oil in the wok. Add the garlic and ginger and stir-fry for 30 seconds.

4 Add the spring onions (scallions), peas, beansprouts, ham and prawns (shrimp) and stir-fry for 2 minutes.

5 Stir in the soy sauce and rice and cook for a further 2 minutes. Transfer the rice to serving dishes.

6 Roll up the pancake, slice it very thinly and use to garnish the rice. Serve immediately.

COOK'S TIP

As this recipe contains meat and fish, it is ideal served with simpler vegetable dishes.

Chicken & Rice Casserole

Serves 4

INGREDIENTS

150 g/5^1/2 oz/^{2}/3 cup long-
 grain rice
1 tbsp dry sherry
2 tbsp light soy sauce
2 tbsp dark soy sauce
2 tsp dark brown sugar
1 tsp salt

1 tsp sesame oil
900 g/2 lb skinless, boneless
 chicken meat, diced
850 ml/1^1/2 pints/3^3/4 cups
 chicken stock
2 open-cap mushrooms, sliced

60 g/2 oz water chestnuts,
 halved
75 g/3 oz broccoli florets
1 yellow (bell) pepper, sliced
4 tsp grated fresh root ginger
whole chives, to garnish

1 Cook the rice in a saucepan of boiling water for about 15 minutes. Drain well, rinse under cold water and drain again thoroughly.

2 Place the sherry, soy sauce, sugar, salt and sesame oil in a large bowl and mix until combined.

3 Stir the chicken into the soy mixture, turning to coat well. Leave to marinate for about 30 minutes.

4 Bring the chicken stock to the boil in a large saucepan or preheated wok.

5 Add the chicken with the marinade, mushrooms, water chestnuts, broccoli, (bell) pepper and ginger.

6 Stir in the rice, reduce the heat, cover and cook for 25-30 minutes, or until the chicken and vegetables are completely cooked through.

7 Transfer to serving plates, garnish with chives and serve.

VARIATION

This dish would work equally well with beef or pork. Chinese dried mushrooms may be used instead of the open-cap mushrooms, if rehydrated before adding to the dish.

Crab Fried Rice

Serves 4

INGREDIENTS

150 g/5¹/₂ oz/²/₃ cup long-
grain rice
2 tbsp peanut oil
125 g/4¹/₂ oz canned white
crabmeat, drained

1 leek, sliced
150 g/5¹/₂ oz/²/₃ beansprouts
2 eggs, beaten
1 tbsp light soy sauce
2 tsp lime juice

1 tsp sesame oil
sliced lime, to garnish

1 Cook the rice in a saucepan of boiling salted water for about 15 minutes. Drain well, rinse under cold running water and drain again thoroughly.

2 Heat the peanut oil in a preheated wok.

3 Add the crabmeat, leek and beansprouts to the wok and stir-fry for 2-3 minutes. Remove the mixture with a slotted spoon and set aside until required.

4 Add the eggs to the wok and cook, stirring occasionally, for 2-3 minutes, until they begin to set.

5 Stir the rice and the crabmeat, leek and beansprout mixture into the eggs in the wok.

6 Add the soy sauce and lime juice to the crabmeat mixture in the wok. Cook for 1 minute, stirring to combine, and then sprinkle with the sesame oil.

7 Transfer the crab fried rice to a serving dish, garnish with the sliced lime and serve immediately.

VARIATION

Cooked lobster may be used instead of the crab for a really special dish.

Fried Vegetable Noodles

Serves 4

INGREDIENTS

350 g/12 oz/3 cups dried egg
   noodles
2 tbsp peanut oil
2 garlic cloves, crushed
$^1/_2$ tsp ground star anise
1 carrot, cut into matchsticks

1 green (bell) pepper, cut into
   matchsticks
1 onion, quartered and sliced
125 g/4$^1/_2$ oz broccoli florets
75 g/3 oz bamboo shoots
1 celery stick, sliced

1 tbsp light soy sauce
150 ml/$^1/_4$ pint/$^2/_3$ cup
   vegetable stock
oil, for deep-frying
1 tsp cornflour (cornstarch)
2 tsp water

1 Cook the noodles in boiling water for 1-2 minutes. Drain well and rinse under cold running water. Leave to drain in a colander.

2 Heat the oil in a preheated wok until smoking. Reduce the heat, add the garlic and star anise and stir-fry for 30 seconds. Add the remaining vegetables and stir-fry for 1-2 minutes.

3 Add the soy sauce and stock to the wok and cook over a low heat for 5 minutes.

4 Heat the oil for deep-frying to 180°C/350°F, or until a cube of bread browns in 30 seconds.

5 Form the drained noodles into rounds and deep-fry them in batches until crisp, turning once. Leave to drain on absorbent kitchen paper (paper towels).

6 Blend the cornflour (cornstarch) with the water to form a paste and stir into the wok. Bring to the boil, stirring until the sauce is thickened and clear.

7 Arrange the noodles on a warm serving plate, spoon the vegetables on top and serve.

COOK'S TIP

Make sure that the noodles are very dry before adding them to the hot oil, otherwise the oil will spit.

Chicken Noodles

Serves 4

INGREDIENTS

225 g/8 oz rice noodles
2 tbsp peanut oil
225 g/8 oz skinless, boneless
  chicken breast, sliced
2 garlic cloves, crushed
1 tsp grated fresh root ginger
1 tsp Chinese curry powder

1 red (bell) pepper, seeded and
  thinly sliced
75 g/3 oz mangetout (snow
  peas), shredded
1 tbsp light soy sauce
2 tsp Chinese rice wine
2 tbsp chicken stock

1 tsp sesame oil
1 tbsp chopped fresh
  coriander (cilantro)

1 Soak the rice noodles for 4 minutes in warm water. Drain thoroughly and set aside.

2 Heat the oil in a preheated wok. Add the chicken and stir-fry for 2-3 minutes.

3 Add the garlic, ginger and curry powder and stir-fry for 30 seconds.

4 Add the (bell) pepper and mangetout (snow peas) to the mixture in the wok and stir-fry for 2-3 minutes.

5 Add the noodles, soy sauce, Chinese rice wine and chicken stock to the mixture in the wok and mix well, stirring occasionally, for 1 minute.

6 Sprinkle the sesame oil and chopped coriander (cilantro) over the noodles.

7 Transfer the noodles to serving plates and serve.

VARIATION

You can use pork or duck in this recipe instead of the chicken, if you prefer.

Curried Prawn (Shrimp) Noodles

Serves 4

INGREDIENTS

225 g/8 oz rice noodles
4 tbsp vegetable oil
1 onion, sliced
2 ham slices, shredded
2 tbsp Chinese curry powder
150 ml/¼ pint/⅔ cups fish
    stock

225 g/8 oz peeled, raw prawns
    (shrimp)
2 garlic cloves, crushed
6 spring onions (scallions),
    chopped
1 tbsp light soy sauce
2 tbsp hoisin sauce

1 tbsp dry sherry
2 tsp lime juice
fresh snipped chives, to
    garnish

1 Cook the rice noodles in a pan of boiling water for 3-4 minutes. Drain well, rinse under cold water and drain thoroughly again. Set aside.

2 Heat 2 tbsp of the oil in a preheated wok.

3 Add the onion and ham and stir-fry for 1 minute.

4 Add the curry powder to the wok and stir-fry for 30 seconds.

5 Stir the noodles and stock into the wok and cook for 2-3 minutes. Remove the noodles from the wok and keep warm.

6 Heat the remaining oil in the wok. Add the prawns (shrimp), garlic and spring onions (scallions) and stir-fry for about 1 minute.

7 Add the soy sauce, hoisin sauce, sherry and lime juice and stir to combine. Pour the mixture

over the noodles, toss to mix and garnish with fresh chives.

VARIATION

You can use cooked prawns (shrimp) if you prefer, but toss them into the mixture at the last minute – long enough for them to heat right through. Overcooking will result in tough, inedible prawns (shrimp).

Singapore Noodles

Serves 4

INGREDIENTS

225 g/8 oz dried egg noodles
6 tbsp vegetable oil
4 eggs, beaten
3 garlic cloves, crushed
1 1/2 tsp chilli powder
225 g/8 oz skinless, boneless
   chicken, cut into thin strips

3 celery sticks, sliced
1 green (bell) pepper, seeded
   and sliced
4 spring onions (scallions),
   sliced
25 g/1 oz water chestnuts,
   quartered

2 fresh red chillies, sliced
300 g/10 oz peeled, cooked
   prawns (shrimp)
175 g/6 oz/3/4 cup
   beansprouts
2 tsp sesame oil

1 Soak the noodles in boiling water for 4 minutes, or until soft. Leave to drain on kitchen paper (paper towels).

2 Heat 2 tablespoons of the oil in a preheated wok. Add the eggs and stir until set. Remove the cooked eggs from the wok, set aside and keep warm.

3 Add the remaining oil to the wok. Add the garlic and chilli powder and stir-fry for 30 seconds.

4 Add the chicken and stir-fry for 4–5 minutes, until just beginning to brown.

5 Stir in the celery, (bell) pepper, spring onions (scallions), water chestnuts and chillies and cook for 8 minutes, or until the chicken is cooked through.

6 Add the prawns (shrimp) and the reserved noodles to the wok, together with the bean-sprouts, and toss to mix.

7 Break the cooked egg with a fork and sprinkle over the noodles, together with the sesame oil. Serve immediately.

COOK'S TIP

When mixing precooked ingredients into the dish, such as the egg and noodles, ensure that they are heated right through and are hot when ready to serve.

Chilli Pork Noodles

Serves 4

INGREDIENTS

350 g/12 oz minced
    (ground) pork
1 tbsp light soy sauce
1 tbsp dry sherry
350 g/12 oz egg noodles
2 tsp sesame oil
2 tbsp vegetable oil

2 garlic cloves, crushed
2 tsp grated fresh root ginger
2 fresh red chillies, sliced
1 red (bell) pepper, seeded and
    finely sliced
25 g/1 oz/^{1}/$_4$ cup unsalted
    peanuts

3 tbsp peanut butter
3 tbsp dark soy sauce
dash of chilli oil
300 ml/^{1}/$_2$ pint/1^1/$_4$ cups
    pork stock

1 Mix together the pork, light soy sauce and dry sherry in a large bowl. Cover and leave to marinate for 30 minutes.

2 Meanwhile, cook the noodles in a pan of boiling water for 4 minutes. Drain well, rinse in cold water and drain again.

3 Toss the noodles in the sesame oil.

4 Heat the vegetable oil in a preheated wok.

Add the garlic, ginger, chillies and red (bell) pepper and stir-fry for 30 seconds.

5 Add the pork to the mixture in the wok, together with the marinade. Continue cooking for about 1 minute, until the pork is sealed.

6 Add the peanuts, peanut butter, soy sauce, chilli oil and pork stock and cook for 2-3 minutes.

7 Toss the noodles in the mixture and serve at once.

VARIATION

Minced (ground) chicken or lamb would also be excellent in this recipe instead of the pork.

Chicken on Crispy Noodles

Serves 4

INGREDIENTS

225 g/8 oz skinless, boneless
chicken breasts, shredded
1 egg white
5 tsp cornflour (cornstarch)
225 g/8 oz thin egg noodles
320 ml/11 fl oz/1²/₃ cups
vegetable oil

600 ml/1 pint/2¹/₂ cups
chicken stock
2 tbsp dry sherry
2 tbsp oyster sauce
1 tbsp light soy sauce
1 tbsp hoisin sauce

1 red (bell) pepper, seeded and
very thinly sliced
2 tbsp water
3 spring onions (scallions),
chopped

1 Mix the chicken, egg white and 2 tsp of the cornflour (cornstarch) in a bowl. Let stand for at least 30 minutes.

2 Blanch the noodles in boiling water for 2 minutes, then drain. Heat 300 ml/¹/₂ pint of the oil in a preheated wok. Add the noodles, spreading them to cover the base of the wok. Cook over a low heat for about 5 minutes, until the noodles are browned on the underside. Flip the

noodles over and brown on the other side. Remove from the wok when crisp and browned, place on a serving plate and keep warm. Drain the oil from the wok.

3 Add 300 ml/¹/₂ pint/ 1¹/₄ cups of the stock to the wok. Remove from the heat and add the chicken, stirring well so that it does not stick. Return to the heat and cook for 2 minutes. Drain, discarding the stock.

4 Wipe the wok with kitchen paper (paper towels) and return to the heat. Add the sherry, oyster, soy, and hoisin sauces, (bell) pepper and the remaining stock and bring to the boil. Blend the remaining cornflour (cornstarch) with the water to form a paste and stir it into the mixture. Return the chicken to the wok and cook over a low heat for 2 minutes. Place the chicken on top of the noodles and sprinkle with spring onions (scallions).

Cellophane Noodles with Yellow Bean Sauce

Serves 4

INGREDIENTS

175 g/6 oz cellophane noodles	450 g/1 lb minced (ground) chicken	2 tbsp yellow bean sauce
1 tbsp peanut oil	450 ml/³/4 pint/1 cup chicken stock	4 tbsp light soy sauce
1 leek, sliced		1 tsp sesame oil
2 garlic cloves, crushed	1 tsp chilli sauce	chopped chives, to garnish

1 Soak the noodles in boiling water for 15 minutes. Drain the noodles thoroughly and cut them into short lengths with a pair of kitchen scissors.

2 Heat the oil in a preheated wok. Add the leek and garlic and stir-fry for 30 seconds.

3 Add the chicken to the mixture in the wok and stir-fry for 4-5 minutes, until the chicken is completely cooked through.

4 Add the chicken stock, chilli sauce, yellow bean sauce and soy sauce to the wok and cook for 3-4 minutes.

5 Add the drained noodles and sesame oil to the wok and cook, tossing to mix well, for 4-5 minutes.

6 Spoon the cellophane noodles and yellow bean sauce into warm serving bowls, sprinkle with chopped chives and serve immediately.

COOK'S TIP

Cellophane noodles are available from many supermarkets and all Chinese supermarkets.

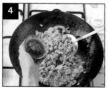

Noodles with Prawns (Shrimp)

Serves 4

INGREDIENTS

225 g/8 oz thin egg noodles
2 tbsp peanut oil
1 garlic clove, crushed
½ tsp ground star anise

1 bunch spring onions
(scallions), cut into
5-cm/2-inch pieces
24 raw tiger prawns (jumbo
shrimp), peeled with tails
intact

2 tbsp light soy sauce
2 tsp lime juice
lime wedges, to garnish

1 Blanch the noodles in a saucepan of boiling water for about 2 minutes. Drain well, rinse under cold water and drain again.

2 Heat the oil in a preheated wok until almost smoking.

3 Add the garlic and star anise to the wok and stir-fry for 30 seconds.

4 Add the spring onions (scallions) and prawns (shrimp) to the wok and stir-fry for 2-3 minutes.

5 Stir in the soy sauce, lime juice and noodles and mix well. Cook for 1 minute, then spoon into a warm serving dish. Transfer to serving bowls, garnish with lime wedges and serve immediately.

VARIATION

This dish is just as tasty with smaller cooked prawns (shrimp), but it is not quite so visually appealing.

COOK'S TIP

Chinese egg noodles are made from wheat or rice flour, water and egg. Noodles are a symbol of longevity, and so are always served at birthday celebrations – it is regarded as bad luck to cut them.

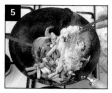

Beef Chow Mein

Serves 4

INGREDIENTS

450 g/1 lb egg noodles
4 tbsp peanut oil
450 g/1 lb lean beef steak, cut into thin strips
2 garlic cloves, crushed
1 tsp grated fresh root ginger

1 green (bell) pepper, thinly sliced
1 carrot, thinly sliced
2 celery sticks, sliced
8 spring onions (scallions)
1 tsp dark brown sugar

1 tbsp dry sherry
2 tbsp dark soy sauce
few drops of chilli sauce

1 Cook the noodles in a pan of boiling salted water for 4-5 minutes. Drain well, rinse under cold running water and drain thoroughly again.

2 Toss the noodles in 1 tablespoon of the oil.

3 Heat the remaining oil in a preheated wok. Add the beef and stir-fry for 3-4 minutes, stirring.

4 Add the garlic and ginger and stir-fry for 30 seconds.

5 Add the (bell) pepper, carrot, celery and spring onions (scallions) and stir-fry for 2 minutes.

6 Add the sugar, sherry, soy sauce and chilli sauce and cook, stirring, for 1 minute.

7 Stir in the noodles, mixing well, and cook until completely warmed through.

8 Transfer the noodles to warm serving bowls and serve immediately.

VARIATION

A variety of different vegetables may be used in this recipe for colour and flavour – try broccoli, red (bell) peppers, green beans or baby sweetcorn cobs.

Cantonese Fried Noodles

Serves 4

INGREDIENTS

350 g/12 oz egg noodles
3 tbsp vegetable oil
675 g/1½ lb lean beef steak,
    cut into thin strips
125 g/4½ oz green cabbage,
    shredded

75 g/3 oz bamboo shoots
6 spring onions (scallions),
    sliced
25 g/1 oz green beans, halved
1 tbsp dark soy sauce
2 tbsp beef stock

1 tbsp dry sherry
1 tbsp light brown sugar
2 tbsp chopped parsley, to
    garnish

1 Cook the noodles in a saucepan of boiling water for 2-3 minutes. Drain well, rinse under cold running water and drain thoroughly again.

2 Heat 1 tablespoon of the vegetable oil in a preheated wok.

3 Add the noodles to the wok and stir-fry for 1-2 minutes. Drain and set aside until required.

4 Heat the remaining oil in the wok. Add the beef and stir-fry for 2-3 minutes.

5 Add the cabbage, bamboo shoots, spring onions (scallions) and beans to the wok and stir-fry for 1-2 minutes.

6 Add the soy sauce, stock, sherry and sugar to the wok, stirring to mix well.

7 Stir the noodles into the mixture in the wok, tossing to mix together well.

8 Transfer to serving bowls, garnish with chopped parsley and serve immediately.

VARIATION

You can use lean pork or chicken instead of the beef in this recipe, if you prefer – remember to alter the stock accordingly.

Fried Noodles
with Mushrooms & Pork

Serves 4

INGREDIENTS

450 g/1 lb thin egg noodles
2 tbsp peanut oil
350 g/12 oz pork fillet
(tenderloin), sliced
2 garlic cloves, crushed

1 onion, cut into 8 pieces
225 g/8 oz oyster mushrooms
4 tomatoes, skinned, seeded
and thinly sliced
2 tbsp light soy sauce

50 ml/2 fl oz/¼ cup pork
stock
1 tbsp chopped fresh
coriander (cilantro)

1 Cook the noodles in a saucepan of boiling water for 2-3 minutes. Drain well, rinse under cold running water and drain thoroughly again.

2 Heat 1 tablespoon of the peanut oil in a preheated wok.

3 Add the noodles to the wok and stir-fry for 2 minutes.

4 Using a slotted spoon, remove the noodles from the wok, drain well and set aside until required.

5 Heat the remaining oil in the wok. Add the pork and stir-fry for 4-5 minutes.

6 Stir in the garlic and onion and stir-fry for a further 2-3 minutes.

7 Add the mushrooms, tomatoes, soy sauce, pork stock and noodles. Stir well and cook for 1-2 minutes.

8 Sprinkle with chopped coriander (cilantro) and serve immediately.

COOK'S TIP

For crisper noodles, add 2 tbsp of oil to the wok and fry the noodles for 5-6 minutes, spreading them thinly in the wok and turning half-way through cooking.

Lamb with Transparent Noodles

Serves 4

INGREDIENTS

150 g/5½ oz cellophane
  noodles
2 tbsp peanut oil
450 g/1 lb lean lamb, thinly
  sliced

2 garlic cloves, crushed
2 leeks, sliced
3 tbsp dark soy sauce
250 ml/8 fl oz/1 cup lamb
  stock

dash of chilli sauce
red chilli strips, to garnish

1 Bring a large pan of water to the boil. Add the noodles and cook for 1 minute. Drain the noodles well, rinse under cold running water and drain thoroughly again.

2 Heat the peanut oil in a preheated wok. Add the lamb to the wok and stir-fry for 2 minutes.

3 Add the garlic and leeks to the wok and stir-fry for 2 minutes.

4 Stir in the soy sauce, stock and chilli sauce and cook for 3-4 minutes, until the meat is cooked.

5 Add the noodles to the wok and cook for 1 minute, until heated through. Transfer to serving plates, garnish and serve.

COOK'S TIP

Transparent noodles are available in Chinese supermarkets. Use egg noodles instead if transparent noodles are unavailable, and cook them according to the packet instructions.

COOK'S TIP

Chilli sauce is a very hot sauce made from chillies, vinegar, sugar and salt and should be used sparingly. Tabasco sauce can be used as a substitute.

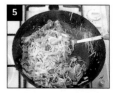

Cellophane Noodles
with Prawns (Shrimp)

Serves 4

INGREDIENTS

175 g/6 oz cellophane noodles
1 tbsp vegetable oil
1 garlic clove, crushed
2 tsp grated fresh root ginger
24 raw tiger prawns
   (jumbo shrimp), peeled
   and deveined

1 red (bell) pepper, seeded and
   thinly sliced
1 green (bell) pepper, seeded
   and thinly sliced
1 onion, chopped
2 tbsp light soy sauce
juice of 1 orange

2 tsp wine vinegar
pinch of brown sugar
150 ml/^{1}/4 pint/^{2}/3 cup
   fish stock
1 tbsp cornflour (cornstarch)
2 tsp water
orange slices, to garnish

1 Cook the noodles in a saucepan of boiling water for 1 minute. Drain well, rinse under cold water and then drain thoroughly again.

2 Heat the oil in a preheated wok. Add the garlic and ginger and stir-fry for 30 seconds.

3 Add the prawns (shrimp) and stir-fry for 2 minutes. Remove the prawns (shrimp) with a slotted spoon and keep warm.

4 Add the (bell) peppers and onion to the wok and stir-fry for 2 minutes. Stir in the soy sauce, orange juice, vinegar, sugar and stock.

5 Return the prawns (shrimp) to the wok and cook for 8-10 minutes, until cooked through.

6 Blend the cornflour (cornstarch) with the water and add to the wok. Bring to the boil, add the noodles and cook for 1-2 minutes. Garnish and serve.

VARIATION

Lime or lemon juice and slices may be used instead of the orange. Use 3-5 ^{1}/2 tsp of these juices.

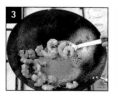

Desserts

Desserts are almost unheard of in ordinary Chinese households and the following recipes are adaptations of Imperial recipes or use Chinese cooking methods and ingredients to produce delicious desserts which would round off any meal perfectly.

The Chinese do not usually have desserts to finish off a meal, except at banquets and special occasions. Sweet dishes are usually served in between main meals as snacks, but fresh fruit is considered to be very refreshing at the end of a big meal.

Rice is cooked with fruits, lychees are spiced with ginger and served with a refreshing orange sorbet and wonton wrappers are sealed around a sweet date filling and laced with honey to name but a few of the tempting treats that follow in this chapter.

Sweet Fruit Wontons

Serves 4

INGREDIENTS

12 wonton wrappers
2 tsp cornflour (cornstarch)
6 tsp cold water
oil, for deep-frying
2 tbsp clear honey

selection of fresh fruit (such
    as kiwi fruit, limes,
    oranges, mango and
    apples), sliced, to serve

FILLING:
175 g/6 oz/1 cup chopped
    dried, stoned (pitted) dates
2 tsp dark brown sugar
1/2 tsp ground cinnamon

1 To make the filling, mix together the dates, sugar and cinnamon in a bowl.

2 Spread out the wonton wrappers on a chopping board and spoon a little of the filling into the centre of each wrapper.

3 Mix together the cornflour (cornstarch) and water and brush this around the edges of the wrappers.

4 Fold the wrappers over the filling, bringing the edges together, then bring the two corners together, sealing with the cornflour (cornstarch) mixture.

5 Heat the oil for deep-frying in a wok to 180°C/350°F, or until a cube of bread browns in 30 seconds. Fry the wontons, in batches, for 2-3 minutes, until a golden brown colour.

6 Remove the wontons from the oil with a slotted spoon and leave to drain on absorbent kitchen paper (paper towels).

7 Place the honey in a bowl and stand it in warm water, to soften it slightly. Drizzle the honey over the wontons and serve with a selection of fresh fruit.

COOK'S TIP

Wonton wrappers may be found in Chinese supermarkets. Alternatively, make 1 quantity of the dough used for Shrimp Dumpling Soup (see page 24).

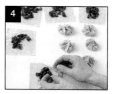

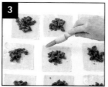

Banana Pastries

Serves 4

INGREDIENTS

DOUGH:
450 g/1 lb/4 cups plain (all-purpose) flour
60 g/2 oz/4 tbsp lard (shortening)
60 g/2 oz/4 tbsp unsalted butter

125 ml/4 fl oz/¹/₂ cup water
1 egg yolk, beaten
icing (confectioner's) sugar, for dusting
cream or ice cream, to serve

FILLING:
2 large bananas
75 g/2³/₄ oz/¹/₃ cup finely chopped no-need-to-soak dried apricots
pinch of nutmeg
dash of orange juice

1 To make the dough, sift the flour into a large mixing bowl. Add the lard (shortening) and butter and rub into the flour with the fingertips until the mixture resembles breadcrumbs. Gradually blend in the water to make a soft dough. Wrap in cling film (plastic wrap) and chill in the refrigerator for 30 minutes.

2 Mash the bananas in a bowl with a fork and stir in the apricots, nutmeg and orange juice, mixing together well.

3 Roll the dough out on a lightly floured surface and cut out 16 × 10-cm/4-inch rounds.

4 Spoon a little of the banana filling on to one half of each round and fold the dough over the filling to make semi-circles. Pinch the edges together and seal them by pressing with the prongs of a fork.

5 Arrange the pastries on a non-stick baking tray (cookie sheet) and brush them with the beaten egg yolk.

6 Cut a small slit in each pastry and cook in a preheated oven, 180°C/350°F/Gas 4, for about 25 minutes, or until golden brown.

7 Dust with icing (confectioner's) sugar and serve with cream or ice cream.

Mango Dumplings

Serves 4

INGREDIENTS

DOUGH:
2 tsp baking powder
1 tbsp caster (superfine) sugar
150 ml/¼ pint/⅔ cup water
150 ml/¼ pint/⅔ cup milk

400 g/14 oz/3½ cups plain
  (all-purpose) flour

FILLING AND SAUCE:
1 small mango

100 g/4 oz can lychees,
  drained
1 tbsp ground almonds
4 tbsp orange juice
ground cinnamon, for dusting

1 To make the dough, place the baking powder and sugar in a mixing bowl. Mix the water and milk together and then stir this mixture into the baking powder and sugar mixture until well combined. Stir in the flour to make a soft dough. Set the dough aside in a warm place for about 1 hour.

2 To make the filling, peel the mango and cut the flesh from the stone (pit). Roughly chop the mango flesh; reserve half and set aside for the sauce.

3 Chop the lychees and add to half of the chopped mango, together with the ground almonds. Let stand for 20 minutes.

4 To make the sauce, blend the reserved mango and the orange juice in a food processor until smooth. Press the mixture through a sieve to make a smooth sauce.

5 Divide the dough into 16 equal pieces. Roll each piece out on a lightly floured surface into 7.5-cm/ 3-inch rounds.

6 Spoon a little of the mango and lychee filling on to the centre of each round and fold the dough over the filling to make semi-circles. Pinch the edges together to seal.

7 Place the dumplings on a heatproof plate in a steamer, cover and steam for 20-25 minutes, or until cooked through.

8 Remove the dumplings from the steamer, dust with ground cinnamon and serve with the mango sauce.

Sweet Rice

Serves 4

INGREDIENTS

175 g/6 oz/^{3}/4 cup pudding
   rice
25 g/1 oz/2 tbsp unsalted
   butter
1 tbsp caster (superfine) sugar
8 dried dates, pitted and
   chopped

1 tbsp raisins
5 glacé (candied) cherries,
   halved
5 pieces angelica, chopped
5 walnut halves
125 g/4 oz/^{1}/2 cup canned
   chestnut purée

SYRUP:
150 ml/^{1}/4 pint/^{2}/3 cup water
2 tbsp orange juice
4^1/2 tsp light brown sugar
1^1/2 tsp cornflour (cornstarch)
1 tbsp cold water

1 Put the rice in a pan, cover with cold water and bring to the boil. Reduce the heat, cover and simmer for 15 minutes, or until the water has been absorbed. Stir in the butter and sugar. Grease a 600 ml/1 pint heatproof pudding basin (bowl). Cover the base and sides with a thin layer of the rice, pressing with the back of a spoon.

2 Mix the fruit and walnuts and press them into the rice.

3 Spread a thicker layer of rice on top and then fill the centre with the chestnut purée. Cover with the remaining rice, pressing the top down to seal in the purée. Cover the basin (bowl) with pleated greaseproof (wax) paper and foil and secure with string. Place in a steamer, or stand the basin (bowl) in a pan and fill with hot water until it reaches halfway up the sides of the basin (bowl). Cover and steam for 45 minutes. Let stand for 10 minutes.

4 Before serving, gently heat the water and orange juice. Add the sugar and stir to dissolve. Bring the syrup to the boil. Mix the cornflour (cornstarch) with the cold water to form a smooth paste, then stir into the boiling syrup. Cook for 1 minute until thickened and clear.

5 Turn the pudding out on to a serving plate. Pour the syrup over the top, cut into slices and serve.

Honeyed Rice Puddings

Serves 4

INGREDIENTS

300 g/10 oz/1½ cups pudding
    rice
2 tbsp clear honey, plus extra
    for drizzling

large pinch of ground
    cinnamon
15 no-need-to-soak dried
    apricots, chopped

3 pieces stem (preserved)
    ginger, drained and
    chopped
8 whole no-need-to-soak
    dried apricots, to decorate

1 Put the rice in a saucepan and just cover with cold water. Bring to the boil, reduce the heat, cover and cook for 15 minutes, or until the water has been absorbed.

2 Stir the honey and cinnamon into the rice.

3 Grease 4 × 150 ml/¼ pint/⅔ cup ramekin dishes.

4 Blend the apricots and ginger in a food processor to make a paste.

Divide the paste into 4 equal portions and shape each into a flat round to fit into the base of the ramekins.

5 Divide half of the rice between the ramekins and place the apricot paste on top.

6 Cover the apricot paste with the remaining rice. Cover the ramekins with greaseproof (wax) paper and foil and steam for 30 minutes, or until set.

7 Remove the ramekins from the steamer

and leave to stand for 5 minutes.

8 Turn the puddings out on to warm serving plates and drizzle with clear honey. Decorate with dried apricots and serve.

COOK'S TIP

The puddings may be left to chill in their ramekin dishes in the refrigerator, then turned out and served with ice cream or cream.

Mango Mousse

Serves 4

INGREDIENTS

400 g/14 oz can mangoes in syrup	200 ml/7 fl oz/1 cup double (heavy) cream	2 egg whites
2 pieces stem (preserved) ginger, chopped	20 g/³/₄ oz/4 tsp powdered gelatine	1¹/₂ tbsp light brown sugar stem (preserved) ginger and lime zest, to decorate
	2 tbsp water	

1 Drain the mangoes, reserving the syrup. Blend the mango pieces and ginger in a food processor or blender for 30 seconds, or until smooth.

2 Measure the purée and make up to 300 ml/¹/₂ pint/1¹/₄ cups with the reserved mango syrup.

3 In a separate bowl, whip the cream until it forms soft peaks. Fold the mango mixture into the cream until well combined.

4 Dissolve the gelatine in the water and leave to cool slightly. Pour the gelatine into the mango mixture in a steady stream, stirring constantly. Leave to cool in the refrigerator for about 30 minutes, until almost set.

5 Beat the egg whites in a clean bowl until they form soft peaks, then beat in the sugar. Gently fold the egg whites into the mango mixture with a metal spoon.

6 Spoon the mousse into individual serving dishes and decorate with stem (preserved) ginger and lime zest. Serve immediately.

COOK'S TIP

The gelatine must be stirred into the mango mixture in a gentle, steady stream to prevent it from setting in lumps when it comes into contact with the cold mixture.

Poached Allspice Pears

Serves 4

INGREDIENTS

4 large, ripe pears 300 ml/$^1/_2$ pint/$1^1/_4$ cups orange juice	2 tsp ground allspice 60 g/2 oz/$^1/_3$ cup raisins 2 tbsp light brown sugar	grated orange rind, to decorate

1 Using an apple corer, core the pears. Using a sharp knife, peel the pears and cut them in half.

2 Place the pear halves in a large saucepan.

3 Add the orange juice, allspice, raisins and sugar to the pan and heat gently, stirring, until the sugar has dissolved. Bring the mixture to the boil for 1 minute.

4 Reduce the heat to low and leave to simmer for about 10 minutes, or until the pears are cooked, but still fairly firm – test them by inserting the tip of a sharp knife.

5 Remove the pears from the pan with a slotted spoon and transfer to serving plates. Decorate and serve hot with the syrup.

VARIATION

Use cinnamon instead of the allspice and decorate with cinnamon sticks and fresh mint sprigs, if you prefer.

COOK'S TIP

The Chinese do not usually have desserts to finish off a meal, except at banquets and special occasions. Sweet dishes are usually served in between main meals as snacks, but fruit is refreshing at the end of a big meal.

Chinese Custard Tarts

Makes 15

INGREDIENTS

DOUGH:
175 g/6 oz/1¹/₂ cups plain
 (all-purpose) flour
3 tbsp caster (superfine) sugar
60 g/2 oz/4 tbsp unsalted
 butter

25 g/1 oz/2 tbsp lard
 (shortening)
2 tbsp water

CUSTARD:
2 small eggs

60 g/2 oz/¹/₄ cup caster
 (superfine) sugar
175 ml/6 fl oz/³/₄ cup pint
 milk
¹/₂ tsp ground nutmeg, plus
 extra for sprinkling
cream, to serve

1 To make the dough, sift the flour into a bowl. Add the sugar and rub in the butter and lard (shortening) until the mixture resembles breadcrumbs. Add the water and mix to form a dough.

2 Transfer the dough to a lightly floured surface and knead for 5 minutes, until smooth. Cover with cling film (plastic wrap) and leave to chill in the refrigerator while you prepare the filling.

3 To make the custard, beat the eggs and sugar together. Gradually add the milk and nutmeg and beat until well combined.

4 Separate the dough into 15 even-sized pieces. Flatten the dough pieces into rounds and press into shallow patty tins (pans).

5 Spoon the custard into the pastry cases (tart shells) and cook in a preheated oven, at

150°C/300°F/Gas Mark 2, for 25-30 minutes.

6 Transfer the tarts to a wire rack, leave to cool slightly, then sprinkle with nutmeg. Serve with cream.

COOK'S TIP

For extra convenience, make the dough in advance, cover and leave to chill in the refrigerator until required.

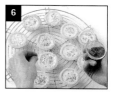

Ginger Lychees with Orange Sorbet

Serves 4

INGREDIENTS

SORBET:
225 g/8 oz/^{1}/4 cups caster
    (superfine) sugar
450 ml/^{3}/4 pint/2 cups cold
    water
350 g/12 oz can mandarins, in
    natural juice

2 tbsp lemon juice

STUFFED LYCHEES:
425 g/15 oz can lychees,
    drained

60 g/2 oz stem (preserved)
    ginger, drained and finely
    chopped
lime zest, cut into diamond
    shapes, to decorate

1 To make the sorbet, place the sugar and water in a saucepan and stir over a low heat until the sugar has dissolved. Bring the mixture to the boil and boil vigorously for 2-3 minutes.

2 Meanwhile, blend the mandarins in a food processor or blender until smooth. Press the blended mandarin mixture through a sieve until smooth. Stir the mandarin sauce into the syrup, together with the lemon juice. Set aside to cool.

3 Pour the mixture into a rigid, plastic container suitable for the freezer and freeze until set, stirring occasionally.

4 Meanwhile, drain the lychees on absorbent kitchen paper (paper towels).

5 Spoon the chopped ginger into the centre of the lychees.

6 Arrange the lychees on serving plates, garnish and serve with scoops of orange sorbet.

COOK'S TIP

It is best to leave the sorbet in the refrigerator for 10 minutes, so that it softens slightly, allowing you to scoop it to serve.

Battered Bananas

Serves 4

INGREDIENTS

8 medium bananas
2 tsp lemon juice
75 g/2³/4 oz/²/3 cup self-
    raising flour

75 g/2³/4 oz/²/3 cup rice flour
1 tbsp cornflour (cornstarch)
¹/2 tsp ground cinnamon
250 ml/8 fl oz/1 cup water

4 tbsp light brown sugar
oil, for deep-frying

1 Cut the bananas into chunks and place them in a large mixing bowl.

2 Sprinkle the lemon juice over the bananas to prevent discoloration.

3 Sift the self raising flour, rice flour, cornflour (cornstarch) and cinnamon into a mixing bowl. Gradually stir in the water to make a thin batter.

4 Heat the oil in a preheated wok until almost smoking, then reduce the heat slightly.

5 Place a piece of banana on the end of a fork and carefully dip it into the batter, draining off any excess. Repeat with the remaining banana pieces.

6 Sprinkle the sugar on to a large plate.

7 Carefully place the banana pieces in the oil and cook for 2-3 minutes, until golden. Remove the banana pieces from the oil with a slotted spoon and roll them in the sugar. Transfer to bowls and serve with cream or ice cream.

COOK'S TIP

Rice flour can be bought from wholefood shops or from Chinese supermarkets.

Index

Index compiled by Hilary Bird.